FRAN'S BED

BY JAMES LAPINE

★

★

DRAMATISTS
PLAY SERVICE
INC.

Playwrights Horizons, Inc., New York City, produced
the New York Premiere of FRAN'S BED Off-Broadway in 2005.

Originally Produced by Long Wharf Theatre, 2003,
Gordon Edelstein, Artistic Director; Michael Stotts, Managing Director.

For Mia Farrow

FRAN'S BED was produced by Playwrights Horizons (Tim Sanford, Artistic Director) in New York City, opening on September 25, 2005. It was directed by the author; the set design was by Derrick McLane, based on an original design from Doug Stein; the costume design was by Susan Hilferty; the lighting design was by David Lander; the original music and sound design were by Fitz Patton; and the stage manager was Scott Rollison. The cast was as follows:

FRAN .... Mia Farrow
HANK .... Harris Yulin
VICKI .... Heather Burns
ROBERTA .... Julia Stiles
DOLLY .... Brenda Pressley
ED/PSYCHIATRIST # 1 .... Jonathan Walker
LYNNE/PSYCHIATRIST # 2 .... Marcia DeBonis

CHARACTERS

FRAN

HANK

VICKI

ROBERTA

DOLLY

ED

LYNNE

SETTING

Fran's hospital room.

TIME

Now and then.

FRAN'S BED

Scene 1

Lights come up on Fran, a middle-aged woman. She wears a dressing gown and sits at the edge of the far-right stage. Across from her, at the very far left, sits Psychiatrist #1. He is in shadow. Between them is a white curtain, a hospital curtain, but in this lighting it might also feel like a window curtain. They speak across the span of the stage as if they're only a few feet apart.

FRAN. *(With difficulty.)* And I'm stranded on a desert island. Somewhere exotic. Maybe Fiji. No, not Fiji, somewhere totally deserted.
PSYCHIATRIST #1. Yes?
FRAN. And I'm lying on the beach and I'm …
PSYCHIATRIST #1. Go on, please.
FRAN. I'm having intercourse with the Secretary.
PSYCHIATRIST #1. The Secretary?
FRAN. Of Homeland Security. I know, that sounds disgusting.
PSYCHIATRIST #1. What happened in the dream?
FRAN. *(Struggling.)* We're having intercourse on the beach — and it was very sandy. Not really all that comfortable. And then just as he's about to reach orgasm — *(She stops herself.)* This is so embarrassing. Why on earth am I telling you this? I don't really —
PSYCHIATRIST #1. Fran, don't censor yourself.
FRAN. I'm very uncomfortable discussing —
PSYCHIATRIST #1. What happened?
FRAN. *(Beat; shrugs.)* I pushed him off of me. I mean, I had incredible strength and I threw him far into the air. He really went flying. Well, this makes him *very* upset, and he demands to know why I did that to him. I told him I don't care for your policies; your

arrogance, your sense of entitlement; and then, then —
PSYCHIATRIST #1. Then what?
FRAN. Then I grabbed his private parts. I squeezed them very, very hard and the Sec — that's what I called him in the dream. The Sec, understandably, he begins to wince and squeak and moan. *(Beat.)*
PSYCHIATRIST #1. And you're squeezing his balls and —
FRAN. Ugh, I hate that expression!
PSYCHIATRIST #1. Expression?
FRAN. I don't care for terms like that. I'm not a prude, but I've always preferred the medical —
PSYCHIATRIST #1. Testicles.
FRAN. Thank you. So I squeezed his testicles and he begs for mercy. Cries for me to stop. And I say: "Only if *you* stop invading my privacy." *(She stops and thinks for a moment; laughs.)*
PSYCHIATRIST #1. *(Beat.)* And then?
FRAN. And then I just let go. I couldn't continue. I was shocked by my own conduct.
PSYCHIATRIST #1. What kind of conduct is that, Fran?
FRAN. Exacting concessions, you know, through the application of force.
PSYCHIATRIST #1. And the Secretary?
FRAN. Oh, he ran from me and dashed right into the water and swam off. Naked as a jaybird. *(Beat.)* He was still aroused … *(Laughing.)* Should I have taken that as a compliment?
PSYCHIATRIST #1. And what became of you in the dream?
FRAN. I woke up. Didn't sleep another wink. *(The lights begin to come up behind the curtain. We see an exact replica of Fran lying in a bed, sound asleep.)*
PSYCHIATRIST #1. How did you feel when you woke up?
FRAN. Exhausted. I mean, the Ambien just doesn't work anymore. Maybe I need something different.
PSYCHIATRIST #1. It's interesting, your dream.
FRAN. They have been advertising a new drug on television.
PSYCHIATRIST #1. There you were, Fran. Marooned on a desert island. Marooned in a seemingly safe place — a place far away from your day-to-day worries. A place where *you* are able to control events, Fran. Able to control *national* events and overcome your sense of helplessness at last.
FRAN. Helplessness? *(An explosion of light and sound as Dolly pulls the hospital curtain open revealing a private and brightly lit room. A television hangs in front of the bed and plays a soap opera.)* I don't feel

helpless … *(Dolly is a Caribbean woman. She wears a white uniform of sorts. Actually, no uniform at all, but rather white clothes to suggest a uniform. On the other side of the bed sits Fran's daughter Vicky. A suburban mom. She knits feverishly, clearly on edge.)*
DOLLY. I don't like that woman one bit.
VICKY. *(Not looking up.)* Who is she?
DOLLY. Just moved to Pine Valley. *(Fran gets up.)*
FRAN. Why would you think I'm helpless?
PSYCHIATRIST #1. Let's not lose the dream, Fran.
FRAN. Sorry, I think we've finished. I have a program to catch. *(Hank, Fran's husband wanders into the hospital room. He looks as if he might have played nine holes this morning.)*
HANK. Any word?
VICKY. Nope. *(He sits and stares at the television for a moment, then dozes off.)*
PSYCHIATRIST #1. Program? *(She wanders upstage next to the replica and watches the television.)*
FRAN. Yep.
DOLLY. Lord, she has the look of evil written all over her. *(Psychiatrist #1 stands.)*
VICKY. I thought you liked the evil ones, Dolly.
DOLLY. *(Taking offense.)* No, I *don't.* It was your mother who loved the mean ones. *(Looking to the bed.)* Isn't that right, Mrs. D.?
FRAN. Well, they're the most fun.
PSYCHIATRIST #1. Why the mean ones, Fran?
FRAN. *(Waves him off.)* I'm afraid we're out of time. *(Beat; he shrugs and ambles off.)*
DOLLY. Oh, she could get all worked up when Maria was bad.
FRAN. Goodbye.
DOLLY. Oh, Mrs. D. Maria's going to get hers this week. I hope you're listening real good to what's going on. *(She laughs at something on the television. Fran has wandered upstage and sits near her likeness in the bed.)* Nothing your mother liked more than a cat fight — *(The phone rings. Vicky grabs the receiver.)*
VICKY. *(Quietly.)* Hello. *(Beat.)* I think he's taking a little nap, Edith.
HANK. I'm up, Vick. *(He rises slowly, creaks over to take the phone in his hand, and retreats back to the corner chair.)* Hi. *(Beat.)* No, she's not here yet. *(Beat.)* I know. She called. Missed her flight but was able to catch another one an hour later. *(Beat.)* Well, then you go. Maybe I'll stop by later on my way home. *(Beat.)* No, don't change

the plans. *(Beat; slightly agitated.)* No, I don't want you to change your plans. *(Beat; he looks to the bed.)* The same. *(Beat.)* I will. Okay. Bye. *(Beat.)* You, too. *(The sound of a car crash emanates from the TV.)*

DOLLY. Oh my, did you see that, Victoria?

VICKY. Now what?

DOLLY. Terrible car accident. I knew nothing good was going to come to them. *(Dolly and Fran laugh.)*

HANK. Could you turn that down a little, please. *(Dolly looks at him coldly for a moment, and then lowers the volume.)*

VICKY. You know, you can go, Daddy. I'll wait for Birdie.

HANK. Don't be ridiculous.

VICKY. You can see Birdie later or tomorrow.

HANK. I'm not going anywhere. Why is everyone always telling me what I should be doing?

VICKY. No one's telling you what to do, I simply suggested —

HANK. I'm staying!

VICKY. Fine, you stay. *(Dolly and Fran let out a big laugh.)*

DOLLY. Watch this, Vicky. Damian is talking Maria through a tracheotomy.

VICKY. How do you talk someone through a tracheotomy?

DOLLY. See, when Maria crashed her car, Cassandra lost consciousness and Maria had no choice but to call Damian — Damian's a doctor and her old boyfriend, and because Cassandra was unable to breathe, Damian has to tell Maria over the phone how to perform a tracheotomy.

VICKY. She just happened to have a scalpel in her purse?

DOLLY. No, but she has a nail clipper in her purse. *(Dolly and Fran howl. Then Vicky laughs, too.)*

VICKY. You've got to be kidding. *(Birdie enters. She is a younger, more attractive L.A. version of Vicky. She wears a chic pants suit, and carries a big Prada bag slung over her shoulder. Dolly turns the volume off. Fran continues to sit on the bed watching the proceedings with a varying sense of awe, amusement and occasional discomfort.)*

BIRDIE. Hi.

VICKY. Hey!

HANK. *(Perking up.)* Look who's here. Sweetheart. I thought you were never going to get here.

BIRDIE. Sorry. Traffic was unbelievable. *(Hugs Hank. He lets out a few sobs.)* It's so good to see you. *(Hugs Vicky. Birdie lets go and turns to Dolly and goes and shakes her hand.)* Hi, Dolly. Good to see you again.

DOLLY. Good to see you, too. Everyone is glad you're here. *(Finally, Birdie looks to her mother.)*
BIRDIE. Oh my God. She looks terrible. *(Emotional.)* I had no idea she was this bad off. Why didn't someone tell me? *(To Vicky.)* She's been like this for almost a week?
FRAN. Has it been a week? *(Vicky nods.)*
BIRDIE. Jesus, it would have been nice if someone let me know what was going on here.
HANK. We thought she would be better by now.
VICKY. We really did.
BIRDIE. Well, when is she going to get better?
DOLLY. Birdie, tell her you're here. Talk to her. Go on. *(Birdie pulls herself together. She goes over to her mother.)*
BIRDIE. Hi, Mom. It's Birdie.
DOLLY. Louder.
BIRDIE. I came from New York to see you. You look good. Are you feeling all right? *(To the others.)* Are you sure she can hear me?
FRAN. I can …
DOLLY. She can …
BIRDIE. *(Back to the replica.)* I've really missed you and — *(There is a ringing sound that startles everyone; Dolly quickly gets up and begins checking the machines that surround Fran. Overlapping:)* What is that?
DOLLY. Let me see. Let me see.
HANK. What's that sound, Dolly?
DOLLY. That's what I'm looking for, Mr. D.
VICKY. Maybe we should call for help.
DOLLY. I don't see anything …
BIRDIE. She looks alright …
VICKY. Daddy, should we get a nurse?
HANK. *(Moves towards door.)* I'll go. *(Birdie is frozen in fear. Then:)*
BIRDIE. Oh, shit. *(She goes to her handbag and rifles through it; finally she pulls out her Blackberry.)*
DOLLY. I never heard a ring like that …
BIRDIE. I forgot my assistant changed it. *(She answers the phone.)* Hello? *(Beat; hushed but all business.)* I can't talk now. *(Beat.)* When? Are you serious? *(Beat.)* Do you know where the hell I am? I can't talk. *(Beat.)* Don't change anything until you hear from me. *(To the others.)* Sorry. *(Birdie shuts the phone.)*
HANK. Is everything OK?
BIRDIE. Earthquake in Tokyo.
DOLLY. Oh.

VICKY. And Tokyo has to do with —
BIRDIE. We're launching our website there today.
HANK. *(To Dolly.)* Dolly, Birdie started a successful website.
DOLLY. Un-huh.
HANK. When she was in college.
VICKY. You already told Dolly —
HANK. Dropped out with her roommate —
VICKY. Daddy.
HANK. What?
VICKY. You already told Dolly.
HANK. No, I didn't. *(Beat; to Dolly.)* Did I? *(Dolly smiles; Hank shoots Vicky a look.)* Tell her the name, Birdie.
BIRDIE. Must we?
HANK. It's cute. Tell her the name of your website.
BIRDIE. *(Embarrassed.)* YouGoGirl.com.
DOLLY. Good for you.
BIRDIE. *(Beat; back to the matter at hand.)* Poor Mom. What do the doctors say?
HANK. She's holding her own.
BIRDIE. When is she going to wake up, Daddy?
HANK. They don't know.
BIRDIE. They don't know?
HANK. The neurologist is going to come talk to us in the morning.
BIRDIE. How could this happen to her? Damn doctors. We should get a lawyer, that's what we should do … *(Vicky and Hank look at each other nervously. Then they settle in. Dolly back to the TV. Hank goes and stares out the window, like a man in a cell. Vicky to her knitting. Birdie at a loss.)* What are you knitting?
VICKY. Sweater for Mazie.
BIRDIE. Hold it up. *(She does.)* That's so cute. Big, though, huh?
VICKY. Not the way she's growing. You wouldn't believe it.
BIRDIE. Where's Mazie?
VICKY. She's back home with the ex-in-law's.
BIRDIE. Why isn't she with your ex?
VICKY. He's at a poker tournament in Reno.
BIRDIE. Why didn't he —
VICKY. Don't ask.
HANK. *(Beat.)* So, how was the flight?
BIRDIE. Long.
HANK. Good food in first class?
BIRDIE. They're always out of chicken by the time they get to me.

Doesn't matter where I'm sitting.
HANK. First class and they run out of chicken!
VICKY. Imagine.
HANK. So, what did you eat?
BIRDIE. Salad, Daddy.
HANK. That's all?
BIRDIE. And I got so lost. What's the deal with the Phoenix airport? *(Murmurs of agreement followed by silence. They are all searching for something to say. Finally:)* Daddy, you look tired.
HANK. I'm fine.
BIRDIE. Why don't you two go. Have some dinner.
HANK. How could I go —
BIRDIE. No, go.
HANK. — you just got here, sweetheart.
FRAN. Just go, Hank.
BIRDIE. Go. Squeegie, leave.
VICKY. Oh God, please don't call me Squeegie. *(They all laugh.)* Does anyone call you Birdie in New York?
BIRDIE. Hell no. I'd kill 'em.
FRAN. They're cute nicknames. *(Dolly rises.)*
DOLLY. Go, Mr. D. You and Vicky go. You've been here all day. Birdie and I will see to Mrs. D. I'm just going to get a cup of tea. Birdie, you want anything? You must be hungry.
BIRDIE. Okay. I'll have a latte.
DOLLY. You mean those potato things?
HANK. *(Laughing.)* Those are latkes. *(They all laugh.)*
BIRDIE. Just a coffee with a lot of skim milk.
DOLLY. Sure. *(Dolly throws Hank a look of contempt, then exits. Hank immediately walks over to the TV and shuts it off.)*
FRAN. Hey.
HANK. Damn thing is on all the time.
FRAN. I was listening to that.
VICKY. Are you staying at the Westin?
BIRDIE. Yeah. Aren't you?
VICKY. I decided to stay at Daddy's. He's never there anyway.
BIRDIE. What? *(She turns to her father.)*
HANK. *(Hank turns to Vicky as if he's just been wounded; beat.)* Let's *all* go out for dinner.
VICKY. You two go.
BIRDIE. I'm staying with Mom for awhile. Besides, I'm on New York time. You both go.

HANK. Come on. We'll *all* go.
VICKY. I want to go back and call Mazie. Just relax. Go to bed early. I'll fix myself some eggs at the apartment.
BIRDIE. Okay, fine. I'll let you know if anything changes here. We'll have breakfast, okay? The Bagel Nosh.
HANK. Oh, the Bagel Nosh. You remembered.
BIRDIE. I'll treat.
VICKY. Well, if you're treating, let's go to Denny's. *(Hank and Vicky laugh, perhaps a bit too loudly.)*
BIRDIE. Go. *(She gives them both hugs and shoos them out the door; a quiet moment with Birdie alone in the room. She goes over to her mother, studies her for a moment. Fran follows her over and sits on the opposite side of the bed.)* This is a fine kettle of fish, Mom. How the hell did this happen?
FRAN. Good question.
BIRDIE. I wish I could do something for you.
FRAN. Me, too. *(Birdie touches the replica's head.)* That feels nice …
BIRDIE. I hope you're having pleasant thoughts … *(Birdie moves to her bag and pulls out her blackberry.)*
FRAN. You're addicted to that thing, Roberta. *(Birdie moves to the corner for better reception and dials. Fran moves toward her.)*
BIRDIE. Hi. Can I speak to Jane. *(Beat.)* Hey. Sorry about before. *(Beat; she looks to the bed.)* Not good. Thanks for asking. Are the Japanese systems back up? *(Beat; steely.)* If it's back up during working hours, we should stick with our schedule. *(Beat.)* Well, let them fucking panic. It's our decision. *(Dolly has entered carrying the coffees, startling Birdie. She looks at her almost embarrassed. She shrugs a "What can you do?" kind of look. Back into the phone:)* Look, I'll call you later, okay? What's the time difference? *(Beat.)* Bye. *(To Dolly.)* I'm shutting it off.
DOLLY. Here's your coffee.
BIRDIE. Oh, thanks.
DOLLY. You're not supposed to use cell phones in here.
BIRDIE. *(Sheepish.)* Sorry. *(She takes one sip of coffee; wincing at the taste, she puts it down.)* Yuck.
DOLLY. It's not that hard to make a good cup of coffee. I'm glad Mrs. D. doesn't have to eat the food here. *(She goes to turn on the TV, then thinks better of it.)* Nothing good on now until *Touched by an Angel.* You know that one?
BIRDIE. No, I've heard of it, but I've never seen it.
DOLLY. It's good. Your mother loves it.

BIRDIE. Really?
DOLLY. Don't you Mrs. D.?
FRAN. Dolly, come on.
DOLLY. She and I would chuckle when we watched it — and sometimes cry. It can be sad. But it's good though.
BIRDIE. Mom cried? *(Skeptical.)* At *Touched by an Angel*?
DOLLY. Un-huh. Didn't you, Mrs. D.? *(Touching her forehead lovingly.)*
FRAN. I know. It's appalling.
DOLLY. Yes, I got your mother hooked on all my programs.
FRAN. Thank you very much.
DOLLY. Well, I guess it's time for her sponge bath. Birdie, you can help me bathe your mom.
BIRDIE. *(Beat.)* Don't the nurses here help you?
DOLLY. Lord, you want *them* doing as little as possible. Besides, they've got their hands full. Come on. *(Birdie moves towards the bed as Dolly pulls the sheet back; Birdie backs off.)* What?
BIRDIE. Her legs — they're not shaven.
DOLLY. Mrs. D. is not exactly going out dancing tonight.
FRAN. This is embarrassing, Dolly.
BIRDIE. I know, but — Mom is so … fastidious, that's all.
DOLLY. I know.
BIRDIE. And her nails …
DOLLY. I'll cut them later. We'll start by changing her nightie.
FRAN. Please don't. *(Dolly goes to undress the replica; Birdie steps away.)*
BIRDIE. *(Rattled.)* I can't do this, Dolly. I'm sorry.
DOLLY. It's still your mother.
BIRDIE. I don't want to see her naked.
DOLLY. She saw you naked plenty.
BIRDIE. It's not the same. I'm sorry.
DOLLY. There's nothing to be frightened of. It's your mother. She bathed you. She cleaned *your* diaper. Now it's your turn, that's all.
FRAN. Dolly, leave her alone.
BIRDIE. No. This isn't what she would want. I know that.
DOLLY. Of course this isn't what she wants. Nobody wants *this* — but this is what God gave her — and gave *us.*
FRAN. I hate it when you get self-righteous, Dolly. Why do you do that? *(Birdie is near tears; Dolly reconsiders her thoughts.)*
DOLLY. *(She laughs.)* Okay, then. You go to your hotel. You must be tired from your travel. You go. It's alright. It's alright. I know it

must be hard for you to see your mother this way. You haven't seen her in a very long time. I totally understand. You go. *(She comes over and gives Birdie a hug.)*
BIRDIE. Thank you, Dolly.
DOLLY. You don't have to thank me. You go. Mrs. D. and I are going to clean up and then watch that angel show. Then I read to her from the Bible.
BIRDIE. The Bible?
DOLLY. Un-huh. *(Beat; Birdie decides not to get into it.)*
BIRDIE. Okay, if you say so … *(Gathers her things.)* Bye, Mom. *(Kisses replica.)* I'll see you tomorrow. You get some rest, Dolly.
DOLLY. Night nurse comes in at nine. Don't you worry about me. *You* get some rest. *(Birdie shakes her head and exits; Dolly begins humming. Humming a pleasant tune. Like there was nothing she'd rather be doing than sponge-bathing a comatose woman. Fran watches with wonderment, then as Dolly pulls the curtain around the bed, Fran crosses downstage and sits. Psychiatrist #2 sits opposite, in shadow. Fran is edgy. Uncomfortable. The psychiatrist speaks in a soft, even-toned manner.)*
FRAN. I am playing at Wimbledon.
PSYCHIATRIST #2. Wimbledon …
FRAN. Right. My partner is the Sec.
PSYCHIATRIST #2. Of Homeland Security?
FRAN. No, this time it was Health and Human Services.
PSYCHIATRIST #2. Uh-huh.
FRAN. And Hank is on the other side playing with the Secretary of the Interior who looks suspiciously like Barb Goodman.
PSYCHIATRIST #2. Barb Goodman?
FRAN. You know, Ed's wife.
PSYCHIATRIST #2. Right. You were playing with them when you fell.
FRAN. Un-huh. So in the dream, I was just amazing at the net; I got to every ball; I was like a wall they couldn't get past. But every time I would serve, both Hank and the Interior lady would fire the ball back with such ferocity that neither the Sec or I could get near it.
PSYCHIATRIST #2. Fran, I'd like to hear a little bit more about your tennis accident. How exactly did you fall?
FRAN. I tripped going for a ball. Everybody laughed at first, but then I couldn't get up. I had this shooting pain down my leg. It really wasn't so funny after all.
PSYCHIATRIST #2. And the nature of your injury was a rup-

tured disc, you said?
FRAN. Right. It still hurts to walk.
PSYCHIATRIST #2. You must be very upset that this happened to you.
FRAN. You know, Marjorie, your tone can be a little annoying. I didn't really come here for a pity party.
PSYCHIATRIST #2. Why did you come here?
FRAN. I came for my family.
PSYCHIATRIST #2. And why did they want you to come?
FRAN. Because they want the old Fran back.
PSYCHIATRIST #2. Don't you want the old Fran back, too? *(Fran just turns away.)* So in the dream, you are good at the net, but not a very successful server.
FRAN. Right.
PSYCHIATRIST #2. Sounds like you could react well when a ball came your way, but when you had to initiate play, you had much less success.
FRAN. *(Whatever.)* Sure.
PSYCHIATRIST #2. And when you were playing with Ed and Barb, did you want to win?
FRAN. Yes. We never could beat Ed and Barb. I would always choke. I wanted to get that ball back on the other side of the net. I wanted to smash it right between their smug, self-satisfied — *(She turns and sees Vicky.)*
VICKY. Good morning.
FRAN. You startled me.
VICKY. I'm sorry. *(Fran turns to Psychiatrist #2 but she is gone.)*
FRAN. I'm so used to having the place to myself in the morning. I haven't been sleeping so well.
VICKY. I thought you were taking something to help you sleep?
FRAN. Can't find anything that works. *(She laughs.)*
VICKY. Sounds like you're exhausted all the time. *(Gingerly.)* Daddy told me what happened the other day.
FRAN. What? *(Beat.)* Oh! That can happen, hun. You forget where you park.
VICKY. Mother, it wasn't the car that got lost, it was you.
FRAN. Well, I took a left instead of a right. I didn't know where I was. It happens.
VICKY. Daddy didn't know where you were. If one of your neighbors hadn't passed you walking on the street —
FRAN. It's easy to get lost in this dreary place. *(She lets out a little*

laugh; Vicky stares at her stone-faced.)
VICKY. You were the one who wanted to move here.
FRAN. I thought we were going to the beautiful Arizona. "The spirit of the West" Arizona. Not the shtetl Arizona.
VICKY. Daddy needed to be near work —
FRAN. I know. I know. I made a mistake. As soon as the rental lease is up, we're going to move to the beautiful Arizona.
VICKY. Well, in the meantime try and make the best of it.
FRAN. I am.
VICKY. Maybe do some volunteer work. You used to be involved in so many activities back home.
FRAN. Right …
VICKY. I hate to see you just sitting around here so much.
FRAN. It's hard to concentrate on so little sleep.
VICKY. Maybe you should see another therapist.
FRAN. *(Not that again.)* Vicky, please.
VICKY. There are a lot of good ones out there if you just take the time to find the right one. I mean, when's the last time you got dressed, Mom?
FRAN. *(Suddenly she bolts from the chair.)* Shut up! Just shut up! *(Long beat; emotional.)* I'm sorry, Squeegie.
VICKY. It's okay, Mom.
FRAN. No, it's not. That's the thing. It's not okay. I can't take it when I feel like I'm being criticized.
VICKY. I'm not criticizing you. I'm trying to help you. That's why I'm here. *(Frustrated, Vicky begins to cry.)* I don't think you even want to see me … *(Fran moves to her.)*
FRAN. Of course I want to see you. Always. I'm so sorry. *(Hugs Vicky and holds her.)* Don't you worry about me. I love when you visit. I wish you'd bring Mazie with you next time.
VICKY. She has school.
FRAN. Why doesn't she ever want to speak to me when I call? Did I do something?
VICKY. No.
FRAN. I don't feel she much likes me.
HANK. Fran, you're talking to yourself again.
FRAN. What?
HANK. You're talking — but you're not talking to anyone. You're talking to yourself.
FRAN. *(Moving towards him.)* Screw you.
HANK. Fine. Screw me. I'd like that. Take off your clothes and

let's get to it.
FRAN. Screw you. I know you, Hank. You think after thirty-three years —
HANK. Thirty-five. Have you taken that painkiller already? You couldn't wait till after dinner? *(Beat; gingerly.)* I'm bringing someone in to help around here — maybe drive you places — *(Overlapping.)*
FRAN. What? I don't need —
HANK. I thought it would be good —
FRAN. That's ridiculous —
HANK. A nice woman from the islands.
FRAN. You went and made this decision without me?
HANK. You'll like her.
FRAN. I don't want anyone around here. And I can drive myself —
HANK. *(As nicely as he can.)* You need to have someone around, Fran, and I'm too busy these days —
FRAN. Ah, you're too busy. That's what this is about. Maybe you should try being less busy, Hank.
HANK. *(He shakes his head and goes back to his paper. Fran just stares at him. After a beat, he looks up.)* What are you doing, Fran?
FRAN. I'm thinking. You should try it sometime.
HANK. Ha, ha. *(Beat; he puts the paper down.)* What are you thinking?
FRAN. I'm looking at you, that's all. I'm seeing the old you.
HANK. Yep. This is the old me …
FRAN. *(Smiles.)* I mean the young you.
HANK. *(He knows what's coming.)* Ah, the young me …
FRAN. *(Coquettish.)* Tell me how we first met, Hank.
HANK. Fran, please. Not again.
FRAN. Come on, humor me.
HANK. We've been through this —
FRAN. I know.
HANK. — how many times?
FRAN. Please.
HANK. For God's sakes, why do you keep doing this?
FRAN. I need to remember. Tell me. *Please.*
HANK. *(Beat; it's easier to just do it; by rote.)* I looked across a crowded room —
FRAN. It was a wedding.
HANK. Why don't you tell it then? If you're going to interrupt me —
FRAN. Sorry. I'm really sorry.
HANK. *(Beat.)* I looked across a crowded room — a wedding

reception — and there you stood — a shiksa princess in a sea of Jews. The most beautiful woman I had ever seen. *(He goes back to his paper.)*
FRAN. No. Don't stop. Please don't go back to your paper. *(She grabs it out of his hands.)* What was I wearing?
HANK. The most beautiful woman I had ever seen — wearing a white dress.
FRAN. *(Their little game.)* Light beige.
HANK. White. At a wedding. At someone else's wedding. You were wearing white. Highly inappropriate. *(Lights change; maybe the room is dappled by a mirror ball; period music slowly builds underneath, maybe The Beatles.)*
FRAN. *(Laughing; girlish.)* It's not white — it's beige. I would never wear a white dress to a wedding, I know better than that. *(She adjusts her robe as if it were a dress.)*
HANK. It's beautiful. I have no problem with it — white *or* beige. *(Straightens his tie.)* You look gorgeous in it. *(He stands; nervous.)* My name's Hank.
FRAN. Fran. I'm a sorority sister of Rosalee's.
HANK. I know. Would you like to dance?
FRAN. Really?
HANK. Yes, really!
FRAN. Thank you, Hank. I would like that. *(Hank takes Fran's hand and walks her to the other side of the stage. They dance.)* How did you know I was a sorority sister of Rosalee's?
HANK. Your name is Francesca Whitman and you're in a Jewish sorority. You're famous in certain circles.
FRAN. I am?
HANK. Indeed, you are. At least among the boys at ZBT. The shiksa goddess of A-E-Phi.
FRAN. *(She stops.)* I beg your pardon. I don't know that I like that.
HANK. It's a compliment.
FRAN. So you say. *(She starts dancing with him again.)* I like A-E-Phi. I didn't join it to be a shiksa goddess. They have the nicest girls.
HANK. I meant no offense.
FRAN. You're not a ZBT boy, are you? I don't think I've ever seen you.
HANK. You haven't. My cousin Howie — over there — he's in ZBT. *(Uncomfortable.)* I'm not in school, Fran.
FRAN. Yeah, I thought you were older. When did you graduate?
HANK. *(He stops dancing; vulnerable.)* Look. I was never a

Wolverine. I went to State. *And* I wasn't in a frat. *And* I never graduated. There, you have all the ugly news. You don't have to dance with me anymore, if you don't want to.
FRAN. Why wouldn't I want to keep dancing, silly! *(She pulls him back in and they dance.)*
HANK. Where are you from, Francesca?
FRAN. Please call me Fran. I hate that name.
HANK. It's a beautiful name.
FRAN. It's a pretentious name and I'm from Lake Forest.
HANK. Ah, Lake Forest ... Your parents must be thrilled you joined a Jewish sorority.
FRAN. (*Laughing.)* I haven't told them yet. I never met a Jew before I went away to school. *(Giggles.)*
HANK. You never feel out of place at A-E-Phi?
FRAN. Oh, I feel out of place mostly everywhere. *(They both laugh.)* You're a good dancer, Hank. You lead beautifully.
HANK. And you follow beautifully. *(They smile at one another.)*
FRAN. *(Looking around.)* I bet *your* parents won't be too thrilled you're dancing with a shiksa goddess.
HANK. They're probably spinning in their graves right now.
FRAN. *(Stops.)* Oh, I'm sorry.
HANK. It's okay. That's why I never finished State. I had to go to work — for my little sister Joan.
FRAN. Oh, I'm so sorry. Well, school's not everything. I'm taking a semester off next year.
HANK. Really?
FRAN. I'm volunteering for Bobby Kennedy.
HANK. Good for you.
FRAN. My parents had a fit.
HANK. *(Beat.)* I don't suppose they *like* Nixon?
FRAN. They love him.
HANK. Yeah. I had a feeling ... *(They dance in solitude for a moment.)*
FRAN. When they drank from the glass and he stomped on it — what did that mean?
HANK. Oh, it's an old tradition.
FRAN. But what does it mean?
HANK. I'm not sure. Something about remembering all the destruction the Jews have suffered through the years.
FRAN. Gosh. That's not a very happy thing to remember at a wedding.

HANK. I think that's the point.
FRAN. Oh. *(Beat.)* I had made up a whole other story.
HANK. What?
FRAN. You know. Something about the fragility of marriage. One false step and the whole thing can just break into a thousand bits. *(Fran leans in and gives him a kiss. He finally pulls away and looks around to see if anyone noticed.)*
HANK. *(Continuing.)* What was that for?
FRAN. I don't know. I think I've had too much champagne or something.
HANK. You should sit down. *(He leads Fran back to her seat.)*
FRAN. I'm sorry your parents are dead, Hank.
HANK. *(Wary.)* I am, too.
FRAN. I think that's why I kissed you.
HANK. Thank you.
FRAN. Thank you for the dance.
HANK. I've never met anyone like you, Fran.
FRAN. I hope that's a compliment.
HANK. Well, yes, I guess it is.
FRAN. Then thank you. *(Hank sits.)*
HANK. And that dress of yours is white.
FRAN. Maybe off-white.
HANK. Maybe very, very "off." *(He picks up his paper.)*
FRAN. *(Smiles.)* Well, maybe … *(Lights begin to restore; wistful:)* How is your Edith? What a name — Edith! Well, I don't blame you. You were lonely. And I'm certainly no company. So you have your Edith now. And I had my Ed. Eddie Goodman once upon a time. *(Smiles.)* Actually, I had Ed Goodman more than once. *(She rises and crosses the stage towards Birdie, who has entered and now sits reading.)* Who would have guessed? We were really invisible people, Ed and me. We never ruffled a feather between us. *(She goes to Birdie; she occasionally slurs her words in this section and moves with an unsteady gait.)* Who have you got, Birdie? I am so pleased, so proud you've become a career girl. But —
BIRDIE. Mom. No lectures, please.
FRAN. I don't mean to be lecturing you, sweetheart. It's just that we used to be able to talk.
BIRDIE. *(Beat.)* Sure, Mom. *(Puts her paperwork down.)* What's up?
FRAN. I worry about you not having a social life, that's all. Working all the time. Being alone. I really don't care who you're with —

BIRDIE. You don't care who I'm with?
FRAN. *(She laughs.)* Of course I care who you're with —
BIRDIE. What are you trying to say, Mother.
FRAN. You're so picky, Roberta. *(Vicky walks into the room with a Christmas ornament.)*
BIRDIE. You don't care who I'm with …
VICKY. Look at this ornament I found. *(Fran moves to Vicky.)*
FRAN. I remember when you two made that.
BIRDIE. Hey Vic, Mom thinks I'm gay.
VICKY. *(Disgusted.)* Come on.
FRAN. I said no such thing!
VICKY. Please!
BIRDIE. Mom *wants* me to be gay. She's so PC.
VICKY. Stop baiting her, Birdie.
FRAN. *(To Vicky.)* I don't *want* her to be gay. Honestly. *(Beat.)* Are you gay, Roberta?
BIRDIE. No. Okay?
FRAN. Well, maybe you should give it some consideration.
VICKY. Mother!
FRAN. All I'm saying is it's nice to have someone to cuddle up with at night. Who cares what's between their legs.
VICKY. Will you two please give it a rest!
FRAN. I want my girls to do whatever they want. I don't want you to live your lives in some fashion just to please us. Never!
BIRDIE. I'm not gay, Mom. However, I am a Republican.
FRAN. No, you're not!
BIRDIE. Yes, I am.
FRAN. No, you're not!
BIRDIE. I am. Conservative!
FRAN. Now you're baiting me.
BIRDIE. I do like that Bush.
VICKY. Yuck.
FRAN. *(Holding her hands to her ears.)* Is that a dirty joke?
VICKY. You are so gross! *(Vicky starts to laugh hysterically. Fran and Birdie join in. She goes over and hugs the girls as they howl; Hank puts down his paper and stands.)*
HANK. *(Rises and stands off to the side.)* Laughter? How dare there be laughter in my house without me?
FRAN. It's so wonderful, the four of us being together again. Like old times.
BIRDIE. How can you celebrate Christmas in such a hot place?

HANK. Roberta …
FRAN. Of course the girls miss the old house, it's only natural.
BIRDIE. We should have kept it.
FRAN. Daddy sold it for me. *(She turns and looks at Hank, then walks over and gives him a big kiss; a passionate kiss.)*
HANK. All right, Fran. Your mother is crazy about me, girls.
FRAN. Your mother is craaazzzy!
HANK. Please.
FRAN. *(Still hugging Hank.)* I love you, Hank.
HANK. *(Uncomfortable.)* I love you, too.
FRAN. *(Taking his hands and pulling him.)* Come on, let's dance.
HANK. Fran, there's no music.
FRAN. We'll make our own music.
BIRDIE. *(Laughing.)* Mom, go get dressed.
FRAN. Girls, sing something so your father and I can dance.
HANK. *(Pulling away.)* That's enough, Fran.
FRAN. *(Moving towards the girls.)* Doesn't anyone in this family want to have some fun? Birdie? *(She goes and takes Birdie into her arms.)*
FRAN. C'mon Birdie, you can be the guy …
VICKY. Mom!
FRAN. Go dance with your father.
BIRDIE. I am a lousy dancer, Mother.
FRAN. Nonsense. My girls move beautifully. *(She laughs and hums and swirls around joyously with Birdie when suddenly she loses her footing and falls to the ground. They all laugh, then Fran lets out a moan and folds in on herself.)*
BIRDIE. Mom! *(She doesn't move.)*
HANK. Jesus Christ, Fran. *(He goes to pick her up.)*
FRAN. Don't touch me! *(Beat.)* I can get up on my own. *(She begins to sob, but then quickly regains her control and tries to get up; Hank just watches her.)*
HANK. Do you now see what I've been talking about, girls?
VICKY. *(Sharp.)* Daddy!
BIRDIE. *(Going to Fran.)* You okay, Mom? *(She succeeds in getting Fran onto her feet.)*
FRAN. Hank, don't talk about me like I'm not here. *(To the girls.)* I'm fine. My back is acting up, that's all. Excuse me. I'm going to lie down for a little while. *(She exits.)*
HANK. You see what I've been living with.
VICKY. *(Taking Hank by the arm.)* Well, you can't embarrass her like —

HANK. Embarrass *her?* You gotta be kidding —
VICKY. You do, Daddy. You have no patience —
HANK. *(Impatient.)* What do you mean I have no patience? *(They begin to exit, arguing, as Dolly enters and sits.)*
BIRDIE. All right, stop!
HANK. Get off my case, Vicky.
BIRDIE. Will you two stop. She can still hear you … *(As they clear, Fran enters from the other side.)*
FRAN. Honestly, Dolly, just go home. I'll make sure you're paid for the day.
DOLLY. I like being here. I like keeping you company.
FRAN. *(Fran wants to strangle her.)* Great …
DOLLY. You should do your back exercises now, Mrs. D.
FRAN. Please call me Fran, and the exercises make me feel worse.
DOLLY. *(Dolly reads from the Bible.)* "The end of a matter is better than its beginning, and patience is better than pride."
FRAN. *(Beat.)* That book is very overrated, Dolly.
DOLLY. That's a sorry thing to say.
FRAN. I didn't mean any offense. It must be nice to have God make all your decisions. That way you're never wrong.
DOLLY. Oh, I've been wrong plenty. He gives us choices and we have to learn to make the right one.
FRAN. Un-huh.
DOLLY. You shouldn't be so fast to dismiss my book.
FRAN. Sure.
DOLLY. No problem.
FRAN. Ya know, I'm just not feeling great today. *(Beat.)* I could really use a Percoset.
DOLLY. Don't you remember? You already had one this morning.
FRAN. Where are my pills? Dolly? I don't appreciate your keeping them from me.
DOLLY. Mr. D. and I just want to make sure you're careful with them.
FRAN. Well, I need another one. Now. My back is killing me. Where are they?
DOLLY. You need to do your exercises.
FRAN. Guess what, Dolly? God is giving me a choice right now, and my choice is to take another pill.
DOLLY. Too many pills are not good for you, Mrs. D. You know that.
FRAN. But the choice is mine. It's *my* lesson to learn, right? That's

what you said. *(Beat.)* Where are the damn pills, Dolly?
DOLLY. I would appreciate it if you didn't swear in my presence.
FRAN. Where are my fucking pills?
DOLLY. *(Calmly reads.)* "All flesh is grass, and all the glory of man is the flower of grass. The grass withereth, and the flower falleth away." *(Fran grabs Dolly's Bible; they struggle over it. Psychiatrist # 1 enters off to the side.)*
PSYCHIATRIST #1. *(Urgent.)* You shouldn't do this, Fran.
DOLLY. Don't do this —
PSYCHIATRIST #1. Don't get upset —
DOLLY. No, Mrs. D. Don't fight me —
PSYCHIATRIST #1. *(Urgent.)* Relax, Fran! Try to breathe.
DOLLY. Don't you leave me, Mrs. D. *(We begin to hear the sounds of her support machines sounding and a growing cacophony of hospital sounds; lights come up behind the hospital room curtain on Fran's family who hover over the bed. Fran lets go of book with an unearthly moan and hyperventilates as Dolly runs off yelling.)* Doctor! I need help. Somebody. Help!
PSYCHIATRIST #1. Try to get control, Fran. *(She starts to silently sob; Dolly races into the hospital room behind curtain with a doctor in tow. They push Hank, Vicky and Birdie away from the bedside to attend to Fran. Lights and sound build, and then suddenly, silence and blackout.)*

Scene 2

Four days later. Hank, Vicky and Birdie sit on one side of the room. The curtain is closed around the bed. Lynne, the hospice representative, stands before them holding a clipboard. Her body language bespeaks the import of her visit. She speaks in a hushed voice and a patronizingly sympathetic tone. She attempts to make this conversation personal, but in fact she does this spiel several times a day, five days a week. This is a job and occasionally she speaks as if she has memorized her lines a bit too well. Like a depressed stewardess. Her detachment, though, must ultimately be comprehendible. Dolly sits off to the side, maybe reading her Bible or just listening.

LYNNE. I know this is a very difficult time for you. Especially to have someone you don't know enter your lives at such a personal moment. *(They nod; Vicky reaches over and takes Hank's hand.)* Please know how sorry I am for you and … *(She checks her clipboard.)* Francesca. *(Birdie laughs involuntarily, taking everyone by surprise.)*
BIRDIE. I'm sorry. Mom hated that name.
HANK. She went by Fran.
VICKY. She does …
LYNNE. *(Change of tone.)* Of course. Fran. Feel free to laugh. I know this is a very sad time — but laughter is part of the life experience, too. It can be a welcome release. *(Birdie stares at her with a furrowed brow.)* The word "hospice" is from the same Latin root as "hospitality" and it refers to a place as shelter and rest for weary or ill travelers —
VICKY. Lynne, we have read the material, thank you.
LYNNE. Oh good. *(She checks her clipboard.)* So, I know you've spoken with Dr. Rosen about the latest tests and the options that you have before you. Unfortunately, as you know, Mrs. Dubin can no longer be kept on intravenous feedings. You have the option of using a feeding peg — that's a tube which is put in the stomach of the patient and which will offer full nourishment. However, Fran cannot be accepted into our hospice care with a feeding peg.
BIRDIE. Because …

LYNNE. *(Making sure they understand.)* Our hospice care is for those who have exhausted all medical treatment. *(Beat.)* We will provide fluids, but of course the body can't sustain itself on just fluids, unfortunately.
VICKY. So basically, Mother will starve to death.
LYNNE. Your mother will be in no pain. Of course, if you wish to continue nourishment —
HANK. We know. We understand.
LYNNE. *(Checks her clipboard.)* Your mother had no living will, I see. Gave no indications of what measures she would have wanted you to take.
HANK. No.
LYNNE. *(Turning some pages on the clipboard.)* I see your mother's state was the result of an overdose of barbiturates which —
BIRDIE. Overdose?
HANK. She didn't overdose. *(To Lynne.)* How can you use that word —
LYNNE. *(Getting flustered.)* I'm sorry. I was just reading what —
HANK. My wife did not take an overdose. She accidentally took too many pills, that's all.
BIRDIE. Daddy, why didn't you —
HANK. Your mother made a mistake, Roberta.
BIRDIE. *(To Vicky.)* You knew about this?
HANK. *(To Lynne.)* Lynne, their mother had been having severe pain issues. She took too many pills by accident, that's all.
BIRDIE. This was *not* an "interaction" of medicines, Daddy?
HANK. I'm sorry, sweetheart, I didn't want to worry you unnecessarily, that's all.
BIRDIE. You didn't want to worry me unnecessarily? Thanks a lot!
HANK. You were so busy and so far away —
VICKY. And what? I'm *not* busy? I'm *not* far away?
BIRDIE. *(To Vicky.)* Why didn't you tell me about this, Vick? *(There is a long uncomfortable silence.)*
LYNNE. Maybe I should come back another time?
HANK. No, we're fine.
BIRDIE. I'm not fine!
HANK. Roberta, stop. Just stop it, okay? This is not the time. *(To Lynne.)* Please go on.
LYNNE. It goes without saying that all efforts *will* be made to see that the end of her life is as comfortable and peaceful as possible. *(Beat.)* Why don't I give you some time to think this over. Here's my

card. *(Checking her clipboard.)* Mrs. Dubin's insurance will allow for her to stay in the hospital through tomorrow, but after that other arrangements should be made. You will be responsible for expenses thereafter. *(They rise.)* Again, I am so sorry. *(She shakes their hands.)* Ciao. *(She exits.)*

BIRDIE. So, is somebody going to tell me what's going on here?

HANK. Your mother over-medicated herself.

BIRDIE. I thought that's why we had Dolly.

DOLLY. Your mother liked her pills, Birdie. They were important to her.

HANK. No one is to blame. *(Dolly sits.)*

VICKY. Oh, please, Daddy. Birdie, she got out of bed one night and took everything she could get her hands on, including some cleaning fluid.

BIRDIE. *(Overlapping.)* Oh my God …

VICKY. It turns out Mommy was having her prescriptions filled more than once and hiding them under the kitchen sink.

BIRDIE. *(To Hank and Dolly.)* Excuse me, but how could you not notice —

DOLLY. I had no idea. She didn't get them from the pharmacy.

HANK. She was buying them online —

BIRDIE. And no one noticed?

HANK. *(Agitated.)* Birdie, what's done is done! There's no point in discussing this now. *(Birdie shakes her head and concedes the point.)* So. Let's get down to business. There's no way we can bring her home.

DOLLY. Mr. D. —

HANK. *(Before Dolly continues.)* I know, Dolly. I know you think you and your sister-in-law can handle it. But that's not what is best for Fran now.

VICKY. Excuse me, but have we already decided that we're not going to give her a feeding peg?

HANK. To what end? So she could live like this? You heard the doctor.

DOLLY. I had a patient once. Everyone thought he was gone — everyone had given up on poor Mr. Gold. *(She moves towards them.)* But he came back. Woke up one day after being in a coma for over *three* weeks. He came back. You don't know.

HANK. *(Polite.)* Dolly, this really *isn't* your business —

DOLLY. That's right. It's God's business.

HANK. *(Agitated.)* And did God decide Fran should drink poi-

son, Dolly? Huh? Answer me that!
VICKY. All right, Daddy.
DOLLY. Mrs. D. drank that stuff because the pills made her think crazy. That night when she first came here — that night when they pumped her stomach — she woke up.
HANK. No, she didn't, Dolly.
DOLLY. Yes sir, she did.
HANK. No, she didn't —
DOLLY. You had already left. She woke up. She said she was sorry. She knew she had done wrong. She asked for my help.
BIRDIE. Dolly, is that true?
DOLLY. As God is my witness.
HANK. Then why didn't you say something? Why didn't you tell me this?
VICKY. Dolly!
DOLLY. It was just for a moment. I rang for the doctor, but by the time he came, she fell back asleep. It's no wonder she's just lying there like that. Why did they pump her stomach if they were going to just start giving her more drugs all over again?
HANK. They were afraid she was going to have a stroke — which by the way, they think she did the other night.
VICKY. Seizure.
HANK. What?
VICKY. *(Impatient.)* The doctor called it a seizure.
DOLLY. That night she came awake — stared me right in the eye — said she wanted help.
HANK. *(Barely containing his rage.)* And you never told us this till now. Why?
DOLLY. I told the doctor. And I didn't tell you because I assumed Mrs. D. would be waking up the next day. I thought she would get better. Everyone did.
BIRDIE. *(Walks over to Dolly.)* And what if she doesn't wake up again, Dolly? What if she just continues like this?
DOLLY. She's like a baby. Like a helpless baby.
HANK. *(Mutters.)* Oh, please.
DOLLY. We need to care for her like a baby you can't communicate with, but you love and attend to all the same.
HANK. Dolly, thank you. We all appreciate what you've done for Fran. Would you mind leaving us so that we can discuss this in private?
DOLLY. No, sir. No. *(She takes her Bible with her and begins to*

exit.) I will continue to care for Mrs. D. whatever you decide. Your mother is a good person. She liked her pills because they gave her some control, that's all. *(She exits.)*
BIRDIE. My God!
VICKY. I don't believe this …
BIRDIE. That woman is nuts. You do realize that, don't you?
HANK. No, she's not nuts. If your mother dies, this woman *and* her sister-in-law are out of a job, that's really the issue.
VICKY. Daddy!
HANK. What?
VICKY. That is so insensitive.
HANK. *(Emotional.)* You think? I think taking that high-and-mighty position that she and her God know best for your mother is what's *insensitive.*
VICKY. All right, Daddy. It's okay. Calm down. *(Puts her arms around him; he starts to cry.)* It's okay.
HANK. I'm telling you girls right now. Don't *ever* prolong my life in a situation like this. This isn't living. Your mother hasn't been herself in years. The doctors say she's not going to wake up. It's time to let her go. Peacefully.
BIRDIE. At home?
HANK. If she goes home, we'll need round-the-clock care. The insurance doesn't —
BIRDIE. Don't worry about the insurance, I have plenty of money.
HANK. I don't want to know about your money.
VICKY. I'll help, too.
HANK. You don't have a pot to pee in. Will you both just stop. *(As he walks and sits.)* Sorry. *(Beat.)* We'll put Mommy in the hospice.
VICKY. Would we keep Dolly on to stay with her there?
BIRDIE. Is that a good idea?
VICKY. We can't stay any longer. We should have someone around Mommy that knows her, right?
BIRDIE. What do you think, Daddy?
HANK. Oh God. I don't know.
VICKY. I think it's a good idea.
HANK. Yeah, I suppose. Dolly likes her Bible. Better that than a bottle of Jack Daniels, I guess.
BIRDIE. Mom did like her, right?
HANK. Who the hell knows what your mother was thinking? So, are we all in agreement here? *(Birdie shakes her head in agreement.)*

VICKY. It's up to you, Daddy.
HANK. Then it's settled. *(Hank walks over and puts his arms around them.)* It's for the best, all the way around. It's the decision I think your mother would have wanted. *(He kisses them both and then walks over to the door.)* I'll go find the salesgirl from the hospice.
VICKY. You want us to come with you?
HANK. No, I'm fine. You two stay with Mommy. *(He exits; the women stand silent for a moment as the lights fade to black.)*

Scene 3

We hear a cry in the darkness. Then another. Or is it a squeal? Lights up on a bed center stage, two bodies cavort under the sheet. We are in a motel room. We hear another squeal of laughter. Suddenly someone pulls the sheet back. It is Fran, ten years earlier, naked under the sheets — very much alive and sexy, bearing no resemblance to the Fran that we have just met. She is laughing hysterically and protesting at the same time.

FRAN. Stop. Please stop. I can't. Eddie, stop.
EDDIE. *(From under the sheets.)* Just relax, Frannie.
FRAN. I'm not in the — STOP! Please. *(She laughs again, then pulls Ed Goodman up. He's an attractive man.)* I'm sorry. Not that. Not now.
EDDIE. Why not? I enjoy it. *(He kisses her.)* There are riches to mine … *(He begins to go back down, but she stops him.)*
FRAN. Will you please stop!
EDDIE. … in them there hills — *(She yanks him back up.)*
FRAN. Maybe later. Not now. C'mon, please. *(She gives him another passionate kiss.)* You bring me pleasure right up here. *(She kisses him again and then they settle in.)*
EDDIE. *(Checks his watch.)* I should have been at my office about a half-hour ago. Ugh.
FRAN. Ugh. *(Ed starts to get out of the bed but Fran stops him.)* Do you like your office?
EDDIE. Huh? I dunno.
FRAN. What's it like?

EDDIE. It's an office, Frannie … What's the difference?
FRAN. I want to picture you there.
EDDIE. It doesn't have much personality. Sort of like this motel room.
FRAN. I like that this room has no personality. We're its personality.
EDDIE. Okay, if you say so.
FRAN. *(Pulling him close.)* I'd like to see your office. You never talk about your work. How did you get into the insurance business anyway?
EDDIE. I just fell into it.
FRAN. And do you like it?
EDDIE. I used to find it fascinating, actually. When I started, it seemed like an almost altruistic profession.
FRAN. Altruistic?
EDDIE. Yeah. You know, if something went wrong with one of my clients, like a fire or flood, a terrible disease — I was one of the first people they'd call. I was there with them, walking through the mess, sitting in the recovery room, straightening out their lives. Yeah, I found it very satisfying.
FRAN. Wow, that sounds really wonderful. But you don't do that anymore. Right?
EDDIE. I'm up the food chain now. It's not as altruistic. It's mostly about numbers and the numbers part of the business is not so fascinating, Fran.
FRAN. Why's that?
EDDIE. *(Change of tone.)* See, the deal with *life* insurance is that you *don't* want people to die. You're betting on them living a long life. You just keep taking their money every month, year after year, and you make the interest off their money essentially.
FRAN. Un-huh.
EDDIE. And the thing is, if you're dealing in *health* insurance, well, it's just the opposite. You *want* them dead — you want them dead as quickly as possible so you don't have to cover extended illness expenses. You want them gone. (*She considers this for a moment.)*
FRAN. *(Dead serious.)* It's an awful business, Ed. *(He laughs.)* Get out right now.
EDDIE. You're funny, Fran.
FRAN. Can't you go back and be the guy walking through the mess, the guy everyone calls when they need help?
EDDIE. On the contrary, it looks like I might be working in Lansing. The main office has made me a very appealing offer.

FRAN. You're going to move to Lansing?
EDDIE. No, I'll commute.
FRAN. That's almost two hours from here.
EDDIE. I know. I need the money. Benjie's got into hot water again. He got picked up last week for pot.
FRAN. Again?
EDDIE. For selling it.
FRAN. Oh Lord.
EDDIE. He just digs himself in deeper and deeper, Frannie. He's driving me crazy.
FRAN. Yeah. Well, he has life, Ed.
EDDIE. What?
FRAN. Benjie's full of life. I like Benjie. He's just too big a personality for this town.
EDDIE. Just a year and a half and he'll be out of school. Isn't that awful — to be counting the days until your kid leaves home?
FRAN. What makes you think he's going to leave home?
EDDIE. Don't say that! There has to be some college that will take him, right?
FRAN. *(Fat chance.)* I guess …
EDDIE. Roberta will be off to school — Benjie will be gone.
FRAN. Un-huh.
EDDIE. I mean Benjie is my only bond to Barb. *(Gingerly.)* It's going to be different for you and me.
FRAN. What are you saying?
EDDIE. We could have a life together then, Fran.
FRAN. *(She sits up.)* What?
EDDIE. Barb and I are never gonna make it —
FRAN. Hold on, Ed.
EDDIE. I know this is a surprise —
FRAN. I mean this has been fun but I'm hardly about to —
EDDIE. Okay, there's no need to —
FRAN. I'm not really thinking about leaving Hank —
EDDIE. Okay, okay. I'm sorry I brought it up. *(Beat.)* I mean with Lansing and all who knows what's going to happen anyway.
FRAN. *(Beat.)* You would really leave Barb?
EDDIE. Yeah. Don't tell me you've never thought of leaving Hank.
FRAN. I made a promise. I made a vow to Hank. It never dawned on me to break it.
EDDIE. *(Duh.)* I think you've already broken it, Fran.
FRAN. *(Nervous.)* That's not the way I see it.

EDDIE. You wouldn't be here if you were happy with Hank.
FRAN. This has nothing to do with my being *happy* or not with Hank. This is something that happened between us. It was exciting and new. I've never been with anyone but Hank. That's all, Ed.
EDDIE. *(Defeated.)* I get the message, Fran.
FRAN. *(Beat.)* Look, let's just not talk about the future, Ed.
EDDIE. *(Curt.)* No. No, you can be sure I won't. *(Long beat; trying to make conversation.)* Are you going to the Franklins' tonight?
FRAN. Oh my God, is that tonight? Another party at the Franklins? Don't those people ever get tired of entertaining?
EDDIE. They like to be the center of attention.
FRAN. Do you think it will be another cheese fondue night?
EDDIE. *(Ed laughs.)* I hope not.
FRAN. *(Fran starts getting worked up.)* Hank loves fondue. And gee, what will we talk about? Which kid is applying to what college?
EDDIE. It's a little late in the year for that.
FRAN. Who's been to which resort?
EDDIE. Yeah.
FRAN. Everyone will tell each other how young they look.
EDDIE. Okay, Fran.
FRAN. The women will admire each other's outfits.
EDDIE. I understand.
FRAN. No, I don't think you do. And there you'll be on one side of the room with Barb, and Hank and I on the other. We're such a cliché, Ed.
EDDIE. Hang on a minute.
FRAN. You and Barb and Hank and me with our fondue skewers poised over a hot vat of cheese.
EDDIE. It's just a party, Fran. *(Suddenly, Fran lets out a loud, primal sob; an almost unearthly sound. Ed, startled, jumps from the bed.)* Jesus! What is it? *(She buries her head in her hands for a moment. Is she crying? She then lifts her head up slowly, an odd, enigmatic look crossing her face.)*
FRAN. Nothing.
EDDIE. *(Incredulous.)* Nothing?
FRAN. It's nothing. I'm sorry.
EDDIE. Christ, we don't exactly want the management taking notice of us.
FRAN. No, that would be bad. I'm so sorry, Ed.
EDDIE. You scared me.
FRAN. I know. I scared myself. I just had this involuntary … urge

to scream. Does that ever happen to you?
EDDIE. No! *(He looks at her warily; checks his watch.)* I probably should get going. We have an appointment with Benjie's lawyer this afternoon.
FRAN. Ugh.
EDDIE. Tell you the truth, Fran, I don't know how we're going to pay for this latest escapade of his. The lawyers and the shrinks are a fortune.
FRAN. *(Dry.)* Don't you have insurance? *(Beat, then she laughs, he doesn't; trying to be empathetic:)* It's just awful. I am so sorry. Come here — let me give you a kiss. *(Ed doesn't move.)* Come on. I'm sorry, Ed. You know how I feel about you. *(Ed moves slowly over to the bed and lets Fran give him a kiss. She kisses him again and then pulls him into the bed. She draws him close bringing his head to her chest in an almost maternal fashion. He submits to the comforts. Fran finally pulls away.)* Okay, do that thing.
EDDIE. What thing?
FRAN. The thing down there that you love so much. *(She giggles, but it is forced.)*
EDDIE. You want me to —
FRAN. I would, actually. I really would. *(He checks his watch, then moves under the covers. We see his body move down the bed as Fran pulls the top sheet around her neck with one hand. She lies back, an inscrutable look crossing her face. This is not necessarily pleasurable for her, but in a valiant effort, she attempts a measure of gratification. Lights slowly change. Hank enters from the side and watches for a moment as Ed disappears into the bed. The lights transform the space into their bedroom.)*
HANK. Fran, are you playing with yourself?
FRAN. God, you scared me. *(Startled, she sits up.)* I thought you were at Joan's?
HANK. We grabbed a bite downtown instead. *(He moves towards her; wry.)* I guess your back is feeling a little better. *(Fran gets out of the bed and begins to make it.)*
FRAN. A little.
HANK. I've never seen you do that.
FRAN. Cut it out.
HANK. You're full of surprises, Franny.
FRAN. Please don't embarrass me.
HANK. You don't need to feel embarrassed. I'm glad to see you're having a little fun in that bed — you've been spending so much

time in it.
FRAN. Hank, stop ... *(He sits on the bed.)*
HANK. No, I mean it. *(Randy.) I'm* here you know. We could *both* have some fun. *(He holds his hand out to her, and she sits next to him.)*
FRAN. I know. I'm sorry.
HANK. You don't have to be sorry. You're always saying you're sorry these days.
FRAN. I'm a wreck. I know it. I'm never fun anymore.
HANK. You're just going through a rough patch. It's okay. *(Caresses her head; nuzzles close.)* You feel good. It's been such a long time since we made love.
FRAN. I'm just not feeling ... *(She takes his hand from her body as if his touch is more than she can handle.)* I just don't feel myself anymore. *(They sit in silence for a moment; Hank is forlorn.)* You've been so patient with me. You've been wonderful really.
HANK. Yeah.
FRAN. *(Beat.)* I want to move, Hank.
HANK. What?
FRAN. I think we should move.
HANK. Move? *(Beat.)* Well, I suppose now that the girls are gone we could downsize —
FRAN. No. Away from here. To Arizona.
HANK. Hello?
FRAN. We're in such a rut. And the doctor said I might feel better somewhere warm. Remember when we went to Arizona? It's so beautiful, Hank. Magical. Don't you want a change, Hank? After all these years — in this house, in this damn town.
HANK. Uh, I feel like I've already had a lot of change, Fran. I feel like being with you lately is about all the change I can handle.
FRAN. I know. That's why we need to live somewhere else.
HANK. I have a job.
FRAN. Your company has two branches in Arizona. I already checked.
HANK. Is this a serious conversation?
FRAN. Yes! Think about it. Think about starting over.
HANK. Starting over? At our age? Is that your idea of a good time?
FRAN. It could be an adventure. We'll be explorers, you and me. My back'll get better; we'll hike. We'll go to unexpected places. Make new friends. Otherwise, what are we looking at, Ed? Just more of the same. *(He sits up. Did she just say Ed? Beat.)* What?
HANK. *(Emotional; not looking at her.)* For the record: I like my

life, thank you. I like the "same." The "same" has done pretty well by us, I would say.
FRAN. We're not the same anymore.
HANK. Yeah, well you got that right.
FRAN. Just think about it, Hank. *(She pulls his face to hers; tender.)* For us.
HANK. Okay, I'll think about it. *(She curls up in his arms and caresses him as the lights fade on them.)*

Scene 4

Back in the hospital room. The curtain still surrounds Fran's bed. Birdie and Vicky sit silently in one corner. Birdie madly types on her Blackberry as Vicky knits.

BIRDIE. *(As she finishes.)* My thumbs hurt.
VICKY. Are you sure it's okay to use that thing in here?
BIRDIE. Why not? Talking on a cell phone is *verboten,* but this is fine.
VICKY. Uh, I don't think it's just a noise issue.
BIRDIE. *(Shaking her hand out.)* I have no choice if I want to have a business to go back to. They're ready to kill me.
VICKY. Yeah, well, I have a kid that hasn't seen her mother in two weeks.
BIRDIE. So, now what are we supposed to do?
VICKY. Now we wait.
BIRDIE. But we don't know how long it will be.
VICKY. Look, I'll stay a little longer. You go back to New York.
BIRDIE. I should be here.
VICKY. You want to be?
BIRDIE. I'd like to be at her side when she dies.
VICKY. Really? Why?
BIRDIE. I don't know. Mom was there when I came into the world, I guess I want to be there when she goes out.
VICKY. Okay then.
BIRDIE. I mean, the doctor said it could be a few weeks. I think they know when the end is close. You can call —

VICKY. I can call? Oh. Well, guess what — I can't leave Mazie much longer. *(She gets up.)*
BIRDIE. Of course. I meant, Daddy can call us both. *(There is a pause, each not knowing what to say to the other.)* I hear these stories of her and the pills and I don't know who they're talking about. I mean she always seemed so normal — of all our friends' parents — Mom seemed the most predictable, right? Eccentric, but predictable.
VICKY. She was president of the PTA.
BIRDIE. *(Going to her.)* Squeegie, do you think she did it?
VICKY. Hmm?
BIRDIE. You know. It must have crossed your mind. Do you think she took those pills on purpose? That she wanted to kill herself?
VICKY. No!
BIRDIE. How can you be so sure she didn't?
VICKY. I won't entertain the idea. I don't want to have a mother that would do that to me. *(Birdie looks and sees her sister's vulnerability for the first time; she goes and gives her a hug. Vicky resists at first, then submits. Setting the record straight:)* I think Mom just lost her balance, that's all.
BIRDIE. Yeah. *(As Vicky walks back to her seat.)* Let's make sure we don't ever lose our balance.
VICKY. We're very different people than Fran and Hank.
BIRDIE. They always seemed pretty happy together, right? Did I miss something?
VICKY. I don't know. Stop trying to analyze everything, please! *(Beat.)*
BIRDIE. Okay… *(She sits; beat.)* You seeing anyone?
VICKY. Yeah.
BIRDIE. Good.
VICKY. Unfortunately, he's married.
BIRDIE. Oh, gee.
VICKY. No, it's fine. Married men are very horny. He's a good interim kind of thing. It's not serious. And you?
BIRDIE. Well … I am living with someone.
VICKY. Oh?
BIRDIE. Or, I should say, someone is living with me.
VICKY. Who?
BIRDIE. This guy.
VICKY. What guy?
BIRDIE. It's so embarrassing.
VICKY. What guy?!

BIRDIE. My personal trainer. He lost his apartment, so I said he could stay with me and one thing kind of led to another.
VICKY. Well, that's great.
BIRDIE. Is it? I don't know — it can't possibly be a long-term thing.
VICKY. You never know. What's his name?
BIRDIE. Jorge.
VICKY. Uh huh.
BIRDIE. Jorge Luis Mendoza.
VICKY. Wow.
BIRDIE. I'm trying to wean him from the gold jewelry and the musk oil. *(Vicky bursts out laughing.)*
VICKY. He wears musk oil?
BIRDIE. Yeah.
VICKY. I'm sorry.
BIRDIE. No. It's pretty hilarious. He's not exactly office-party material. And he got me pregnant.
VICKY. What?
BIRDIE. I took care of it.
VICKY. Birdie, I'm so sorry. I wish you had called. *(She moves to hug Birdie.)*
BIRDIE. Let's not make a drama of it.
VICKY. I wasn't making a drama. I just —
BIRDIE. Forget it. Forget I even said anything.
VICKY. *(Beat.)* Forgotten. *(Beat.)* This place is freaking me out. I don't know how much more I can take. I just want it to be over. Isn't that terrible?
BIRDIE. *(Beat.)* Maybe you should get out of here for a while, Vick.
VICKY. No.
BIRDIE. There's nothing more we can do for her now. We should *both* go back home. That's what Mom would have wanted.
VICKY. You think?
BIRDIE. Yes. Daddy will call us. *(Vicky nods; Birdie gives her a desperate hug, then pulls away.)*
VICKY. You're right. I've got to get out of here. I'm going for a walk.
BIRDIE. If you wait till Dolly comes back, I'll go with you.
VICKY. Actually, I'd like some time to myself.
BIRDIE. *(Hiding her disappointment.)* Sure. Of course. You've been just great through all of this.
VICKY. Thanks. *(Vicky smiles weakly and exits; Birdie stands, lost for a moment, then pulls the curtain back. She goes to Fran's bedside and takes her hand.)*

BIRDIE. Hey, Mom. I guess I'm going back to New York tomorrow. Work, you know. I've got news! I just started another company, how about that? I didn't want to tell Daddy, he makes such a big deal of things. I hate when he brags. And I always feel like it makes Squeegie jealous or something. Still, the news made the *Wall Street Journal*. How about that? *(Beat; suddenly emotional.)* It sure would have been nice to share that news with you. Not to mention the next thirty years or so … *(Beat; from a deep, angry place.)* I really wish you hadn't done this. *(Lynne knocks on the door.)*

LYNNE. Hi. Is your father around?

BIRDIE. Nope.

LYNNE. Oh. Well, I know you've made your decision. It's a good thing you didn't let it drag out too long. This is never an easy time.

BIRDIE. Thank you.

LYNNE. So. I have the papers here.

BIRDIE. Thanks.

LYNNE. Any family member can sign. *(Hands her the paperwork.)*

BIRDIE. Oh …

LYNNE. I have to be the witness. I can't just leave them. *(Checks her watch.)* Unfortunately, I have to pick my kid up at school. *(Her tone becomes more conversational, as if she's grateful to have someone to chat with.)* My son usually goes home with our neighbors' kids but he had a fight today with their older boy so now he won't step foot in their car. It's not really his fault. Joey picks on him. That kid is a bit of a psycho. You have kids?

BIRDIE. No. No, I don't.

LYNNE. *(Beat.)* Well, I can come back.

BIRDIE. I'll sign them now.

LYNNE. Really? Okay. Good. Thank you. *(Lynne puts the clipboard in front of Birdie and shows her where to sign.)* This one. That says you're opting for hospice care in one of our facilities. *(Birdie signs.)* And this one here — that says that we won't be taking any measures to resuscitate the patient. Should any emergency arise, no efforts will be made to prolong her life. *(Birdie pauses. The enormity of the situation finally hits her. She turns to stare at her mother.)* If you don't want to sign it right now, that's okay. A lot of people have a hard time — *(Birdie signs.)* Oh, and just initial here please. That says you've declined the feeding peg. Again, I truly am sorry. I'm sure she was a wonderful mother. *(Birdie looks at her, then signs the second page.)* And here's the financial agreement.

BIRDIE. I'll take care of the deposit and the first month now.

(Reaches for her checkbook.)
LYNNE. Oh, your father gave me his credit card number —
BIRDIE. That's all right. Don't use it. I'll write you a check. *(She begins to write the check.)*
LYNNE. But I think he wanted the miles. *(Beat; Birdie then stops writing and looks at her incredulously.)*
BIRDIE. What did you say?
LYNNE. *(Rattled.)* People often, you know, prefer using a card … *(Birdie bursts into tears, then quickly pulls herself together. She finishes writing the check then hands it to Lynne along with a business card.)*
BIRDIE. *(Avoiding eye contact.)* Here's the check. Just send me the bills directly from now on.
LYNNE. Sure. I'm so sorry.
BIRDIE. *(Looking away.)* Thank you.
LYNNE. *(Separating the pages like a car rental form.)* Here are your copies. *(She takes the others and puts them in her clipboard. Checks her watch.)* There doesn't seem to be enough hours in the day. God bless. *(Lynne exits; Birdie sits for a moment looking at the contracts. Dinner bell rings. Fran enters. Perhaps lights and sound effects communicate the dreamlike quality of this flashback:)*
FRAN. Where is everyone? The food is going to get cold. *(Calling off.)* Hank! Squeegie! *(Fran arranges the chairs.)* Birdie, put away your work please.
BIRDIE. I wish they'd hurry. This paper is due tomorrow.
FRAN. What's it on, darling?
BIRDIE. "The Death of Ivan Ilyich." What a bore. *(Hank enters.)*
HANK. Smells good, Frannie.
FRAN. Where is Vicky? *(Calls off; Hank sits.)* Victoria — come on! *(Vicky enters.)*
VICKY. I'm here. I'm here. You don't have to yell.
FRAN. I wasn't yelling. *(To Hank.)* Was I yelling? *(He ignores her.)* Well, sit down.
HANK. Mmm, Fran's special shepherd's pie.
VICKY. Not with the lamb, I hope.
FRAN. I haven't made it with lamb in years. Birdie, stop reading and serve yourself.
VICKY. Do you have a test?
BIRDIE. Tolstoy's short stories.
HANK. Sounds important.
FRAN. I think I read the "Ilyich" one in college …
BIRDIE. I don't know why I ever took AP English.

FRAN. Because your advisor told you —
HANK. You're smart. That's why you're in with all the older kids.
BIRDIE. I'm only smart in math and science. I can't write worth crap.
FRAN. Must you use that word at the dinner table?
BIRDIE. Does this have lamb in it?
FRAN. What is it with the two of you and lamb?
BIRDIE. You sneak it in sometimes thinking we won't notice.
VICKY. And then it repeats on us all night.
FRAN. That was just one time and it was because I ran out of beef. Will you get off my case?
HANK. It's delicious.
FRAN. Thank you, honey. At least someone appreciates my efforts.
HANK. Pass the broccoli.
FRAN. Vicky, you haven't taken anything. Aren't you hungry? Do you want something else?
VICKY. I had a snack at Cooper's after school.
BIRDIE. Ewww, Cooper's. That place is vermin-ridden.
VICKY. Yeah, that was my snack. Vermin. *(They sit in silence.)*
FRAN. I have an idea. This Saturday is Earth Day. There's a big fair down in Detroit and I thought we could all go and then on the drive back we could pick strawberries, like we used to. Wouldn't that be fun? *(They stare at her; no response.)* Maybe have dinner at that inn that's owned by the Mennonites? *(Beat; still no response.)* Remember, the one we always used to go to when you were little?
BIRDIE. *(Finally.)* Ah, sorry, Mom. I've got plans Saturday.
FRAN. What?
BIRDIE. Plans. As in other things to do.
FRAN. What plans?
BIRDIE. Does everyone always have to know everything about me?
HANK. Yes. What plans?
BIRDIE. I've got a date.
FRAN. You do? How exciting. Who's the lucky boy?
BIRDIE. Well, not exactly a date. I'm getting together with someone. *(Beat.)*
HANK. Just tell us who you're getting together with, Birdie.
BIRDIE. Peter.
VICKY. Which Peter?
BIRDIE. Knipe. He asked me to the baseball game and then the party afterwards.
HANK. How are you getting there?

BIRDIE. He's going to drive me, of course.
FRAN. *(Defeated.)* He's a senior, Hank.
HANK. You're not driving with him. I'll drive you both.
BIRDIE. Daddy! Don't be ridiculous.
HANK. You're just a freshman, Birdie. The rule is you have to be a junior, you know that. Your sister can drive you then.
VICKY. *(Gets up in a huff.)* Did it ever occur to you to ask me first before you offer up my services?
FRAN. Victoria, where are you going?
VICKY. I'm done.
FRAN. You didn't eat anything. Not a single bite. And we haven't finished. Now sit down please.
VICKY. I don't feel well.
FRAN. Oh Vicky. We have to get you to a doctor.
VICKY. I don't need a doctor.
FRAN. You've been complaining about your tummy now for —
VICKY. My tummy? My tummy? What am I, nine?
BIRDIE. If you care, Vicky, I won't go. I didn't know what to say. He just asked me out of the blue. I was taken completely off-guard. The guy's a nerd anyway.
VICKY. Oh just shut up! You're such a frickin' bitch sometimes!
FRAN. Hey, language!
HANK. What is going on here?
VICKY. You all make me sick. *(She runs out of the room; we hear a loud door slam.)*
FRAN. Victoria!
HANK. Will someone please explain to me what is going on?
FRAN. Birdie. Really.
BIRDIE. What? Fine, I won't go. I don't even like him. He just has a nice car. I won't go. Okay, everybody happy? Let's go pick strawberries with the Mennonites. That sounds like fun. *(Mocking.)* May I please be excused from the table?
FRAN. No, Birdie, you may not.
BIRDIE. Don't Birdie me, Mother.
HANK. Will someone please tell me —
BIRDIE. *(Getting worked up.)* You treat us both like children.
FRAN. Well, then don't act like children! I was hoping we could spend a little time together —
BIRDIE. We spend plenty of time together. And we have nothing to talk about. So why don't you two go strawberry picking! Why don't you two go do something together for once. Talk to each

other and leave Vicky and I out of it for a change! *(She gets up and storms out, screaming; door slam.)*

HANK. What the hell —

FRAN. This is some boy that Vicky has a little crush on.

HANK. Well, if he asked Birdie out —

FRAN. She could have said no. She could have thought how her sister might have felt.

HANK. Oh, come on. You heard her say she was taken off-guard.

FRAN. You never back me up, Hank. Never! Vicky hasn't had a date since last summer.

HANK. Leave her alone. So what if she hasn't had a date recently. Just stop worrying about the girls —

FRAN. Someone around here has to —

HANK. Ah, there it is …

FRAN. You're never around for them.

HANK. I'm around. I was just trying to have some dinner with them in fact —

FRAN. But you don't talk to them.

HANK. Who can talk to them? They don't want to give us the time of day. It's a phase. And if you would try and stop controlling their lives —

FRAN. I don't try to control their lives —

HANK. Yeah, you do! You have a master plan for all occasions, Fran.

FRAN. I want to be involved, that's all. Excuse me for wanting to have a little interaction with someone in this house. *(He stands.)*

HANK. Jesus, what is it? Are you all having your period at the same time?

FRAN. That's disgusting.

HANK. Oh, please. *(He starts to leave.)*

FRAN. Where are you going?

HANK. To pick strawberries, Fran. *(He storms out.)*

FRAN. And I suppose I have to clean up the kitchen now? *(Mutters to herself with a smirk.)* And I'm glad I put lamb in the shepherd's pie. *(Psychiatrist #1 enters.)*

PSYCHIATRIST #1. Good morning.

FRAN. Good morning.

PSYCHIATRIST #1. Have a seat. *(Casual.)* Fran, I'd like to start the day with a request, if I may.

FRAN. Request? What kind of request?

PSYCHIATRIST #1. I would like your permission to speak with your butcher.

FRAN. My butcher? Why?
PSYCHIATRIST #1. I just want to touch base with him about the products you're using. *(Beat.)* Do you have a problem with that?
FRAN. Did my husband call you?
PSYCHIATRIST #1. *(Beat.)* Yes, in fact he did.
FRAN. *(Angry.)* You're not supposed to speak with *him.*
PSYCHIATRIST #1. I would never divulge anything that transpires in this room. Your husband's concerned you're mixing your ingredients and not following your recipes.
FRAN. I won't give you permission to speak to my butcher. Or my husband.
PSYCHIATRIST #1. May I ask why?
FRAN. I am tired of being treated like some kind of child. I can handle myself. I know my way around a kitchen. Contrary to whatever Hank thinks, I can deal with my own ingredients.
PSYCHIATRIST #1. I didn't mean to make you feel like a child.
FRAN. *(She rises.)* Stupid game.
PSYCHIATRIST #1. Hmm?
FRAN. I should never have gone for that ball. I never should have played tennis in the first place.
PSYCHIATRIST #1. I'm not following you —
FRAN. Oh, you follow just fine!
PSYCHIATRIST #1. Have you in fact really gone off the Vicodin?
FRAN. *(Stunned.)* Yes! *(Beat; uncomfortable.)* Okay, so the doctor ended up giving me a different pill instead. I didn't tell you that. But you didn't ask, either. I didn't actually lie to you.
PSYCHIATRIST #1. I never said you lied.
FRAN. *(Deeply upset.)* The implication was clear. This is so embarrassing. Excuse me. *(Starts to leave; explosion of light and sound as the hospital curtain flies open. Hank, Vicky and Birdie enter right in Fran's path. Vicky and Birdie are dressed to leave. They say their hellos as Dolly shuts off the television.)*
PSYCHIATRIST #1. Fran, I wouldn't leave just yet.
HANK. We went over to the new place. I thought Fran would have been moved by now.
FRAN. Am I moving?
HANK. Didn't they say first thing this morning?
DOLLY. Yes, they did. I've been waiting, but nobody's showed up.
HANK. They had no info at the hospice. I left a message for the lady.
VICKY. Mom looks peaceful today. *(She and Birdie move over to the bed.)*

BIRDIE. Hi, Mom. Vick and I are going home, but we'll be back.
VICKY. Hi, Mommy. I'm just going to go home to Michigan and check in on Mazie for a while, and then I'll be here before you know it.
FRAN. My girls are leaving? *(She gets lost in thought.)*
BIRDIE. Daddy will be here with you. And Dolly. *(Hank moseys over.)*
HANK. Yeah, you're right, she does look peaceful, Vick. She's probably happy to have those tubes out of her arms. *(He kisses Fran on the forehead.)* Well, Frannie dear, you've got your sleep now. Of course, *we* haven't slept in two weeks ...
PSYCHIATRIST #1. What are you thinking, Fran?
FRAN. Why am I here? *(The telephone rings. Vicky quickly picks it up.)*
VICKY. Hello? Hi Edith. *(Beat.)* Yes, we are about to go home. *(Beat.)* I'm not being an angel. Your kids will do the same for you. *(Beat.)* Well of course, I hope you don't. *(Beat.)* Yes, I know you won't. *(Beat.)* Yes, may you go in your sleep. Then again, you may not. And please, don't call my mother's room again! It's inappropriate. *(She slams the phone down; to Hank.)* Edith called. *(Hank stares at her coldly.)*
FRAN. I hate Edith and I hate you too, Hank. How dare you call my shrink.
PSYCHIATRIST #1. I think he was worried about you; you can understand that. *(Lynne rushes in, clipboard in hand.)*
HANK. There you are. We thought Fran was going to be moved this morning.
LYNNE. I am *so* sorry. You're right, that was the plan. *(Fran is no longer watching the proceedings.)*
PSYCHIATRIST #1. Fran? Maybe you should listen to this.
FRAN. What?
PSYCHIATRIST #1. You need to hear what's happening. *(Fran turns her attention upstage.)*
LYNNE. We've hit a little snag.
HANK. Snag. What do you mean, snag?
FRAN. Snag? *(They all look to one another alarmed, then:)*
LYNNE. It seems that our hospice can't admit Mrs. Dubin today.
VICKY. Why?
HANK. What is going on here?
FRAN. What *is* going on here?
PSYCHIATRIST #1. If you're going to wake up, Fran, this would be a good time. *(She moves upstage.)*

LYNNE. Well, there are new regulations before you can cease life support, and it seems the paperwork has not been processed.
BIRDIE. You have got to be kidding.
HANK. I don't believe what I'm hearing.
VICKY. Well, when will they process the paperwork?
LYNNE. My supervisor is looking into it. She thinks because of Mrs. Dubin's young age, it could take as long as a week —
BIRDIE. A week? How could it take that long?
LYNNE. Well, to be perfectly honest, I hear that certain appointed officials will take as much time as they can to do the processing.
VICKY. What do you mean?
HANK. What officials?
FRAN. What officials?
LYNNE. It's their way of trying to get you to reconsider your decision. They may want to speak with you in person before they sign off on releasing Mrs. Dubin.
HANK. Goddamn them. It's not enough what we've been through? *(He plops into the chair.)*
VICKY. What about Mom?
FRAN. *(Sadly.)* Yeah. What about Mom? *(She looks to the psychiatrist, but he has disappeared; she goes upstage and sits by her replica.)*
LYNNE. The hospital will immediately put the patient back on tubal nourishment until she is cleared into our care.
HANK. *(Angry.)* Didn't you know this might happen, Lynne?
LYNNE. *(Emotional.)* Like I said, the regulations have recently changed —
HANK. It is your job to know about these things.
LYNNE. I have only been doing this for a month, sir.
HANK. Couldn't your supervisor have warned us, huh?
LYNNE. *(To the girls.)* This job is way too stressful. I am going back into sales just as soon as I can find an opening with flexible hours and benefits. *(To Hank.)* You think I like doing this? *(Lynne flees the room.)*
VICKY. What do you think we should do now? *(Hank buries his head in his lap.)*
HANK. Let's go. You'll miss your planes.
BIRDIE. We can't go now.
HANK. Yes, you can. I'll deal with this. You've put your lives on hold long enough. I'll figure this out.
VICKY. But Daddy, we wanted to be there when she was moved —
HANK. *(As he heads to the door.)* Let's go!

VICKY. I really think one of us should stay with —
HANK. Now! *(He exits; the girls look at one another.)*
BIRDIE. This is going to push him right over the edge.
DOLLY. You better go. *(They kiss their mother goodbye.)*
BIRDIE. Goodbye, Dolly. Bye Mom.
VICKY. Take care of Mommy.
DOLLY. You know I will. *(They give her hugs and leave; Fran watches them leave. She goes to the replica and fusses with her for a moment.)* It's all going to be okay, Mrs. D. It's all going to turn out fine. Just you and me now.
FRAN. *(Sadly.)* Just you and me now?
DOLLY. Let's see if we can find our story. *(She turns on the television and surfs a few channels before settling in; both she and Fran stare at the screen; we hear the familiar sounds of the soap opera's theme, then Fran's voice emanating from the television. Offstage:)* The girls are here. We're still waiting for Mr. Dubin. *(Lights change. Video sequence: The television swivels around; we see Fran on the screen. She is in a gorgeous white peignoir and coiffed to the max, sitting behind a desk in a well-appointed room. Dolly stands at her side. She is done up in executive secretary mode. Dolly walks to the door and Vicky and Roberta enter. They wear a bit too much makeup. Everything is slightly off, even by soap opera standards. Note: The first half of the scene is shot in brightly lit soap opera fashion. The second half might bleed to a moodier black and white look. [It is also possible to do this sequence live onstage with a simple change of lighting, sound and costumes.])*
FRAN. Thank you for coming, girls.
VICKY. *(Cold.)* What is this about, Mother?
FRAN. There's been a turn of events I think you should know about.
BIRDIE. Turn of events?
FRAN. I have decided, since your father and I have separated, that there should be an amendment of my financial arrangements with the family.
DOLLY. *(As she watches the program.)* Oh, here it comes. I knew she would get her revenge.
VICKY. Mother, can we not have another one of your little dramas? Just tell us why you've called us here.
DOLLY. I think you girls should show your mother the respect she deserves.
BIRDIE. I haven't said a thing.
FRAN. I want you to sign your shares of Dubin Biotech over to me.

VICKY. What! That's ridiculous.
BIRDIE. Does Father know about this?
FRAN. It doesn't matter what your father knows. I've given my life to this business. I've more than paid my dues around here. And now, I deserve to be the sole controlling interest.
BIRDIE. What's to become of Daddy?
FRAN. Daddy? The matter is out of his hands.
VICKY. *(Scoffs.)* You think I'm going to sign over my shares to you just like that?
FRAN. No, Victoria, but if you don't, then I will have no choice but to ask you to submit to a DNA test; you just might find you have no legal right to those shares —
VICKY. What are you saying?
FRAN. I think you know what I'm saying …
BIRDIE. Mother!
DOLLY. *(Laughing.)* I knew that Vicky wasn't his.
VICKY. You're evil, and you're out of your mind.
FRAN. On the contrary. I've never felt more clear-headed.
DOLLY. Alright!
FRAN. Well, Roberta? You've been unusually quiet through all of this.
VICKY. Quiet like a fox. *(Birdie shoots her a look.)*
BIRDIE. *(Emotional.)* I don't always approve of your behavior, Mother, but I love you all the same. I don't care about your money, I care about you and if this is what you want, what you need, then my shares are yours.
FRAN. Roberta, wipe away those tears. And don't ever use your emotions to win a point. I want to see you be strong. And I certainly don't want tear stains on this document! *(She winks at Birdie.)* Now, come over here and sign. *(Fran gives a little smile and Birdie walks over to sign the papers. Just as she's about to sign:)*
HANK. Stop! Don't do that, Roberta! *(All eyes on Hank, who stands in the doorway.)*
FRAN. Well, look what the cat dragged in.
HANK. Ha ha. I resent what you are doing to our girls, Francesca.
FRAN. *Our* girls?
HANK. You know they are. And there will be no exacting of concessions through the application of force in this family!
FRAN. *(Beat; dropping character.)* Cut! Why isn't anyone looking at me? Are you all so unprofessional that you have to read every one of your lines off the teleprompter? *(Fran walks downstage towards the*

television. The hospital room disappears. They continue staring right past Fran onscreen. She turns slowly to look at the teleprompter. She sees herself on the screen. The Fran we know, looking pale and haunted, staring back bewildered:) What is going on? *(In black and white, the characters now stare down at her from the television:)*
HANK. We're all waiting to make sense of the ending, Fran.
BIRDIE. Did you mean to kill yourself, Mom?
VICKY. Birdie, stop. Leave her alone.
HANK. No. I think we all need to know that. Did you, Fran?
FRAN. *(Surprised.)* Kill myself?
HANK. Yes.
VICKY. Mommy was in pain. She couldn't sleep. She took too many pills by accident. Why is that so hard for everyone to accept?
BIRDIE. Because she washed them down with cleaning fluid.
VICKY. If Mommy meant to kill herself, she would have left a note, right?
FRAN. Right.
BIRDIE. The fact remains, Mommy did this to herself whether she meant to or not.
FRAN. Right.
HANK. I should never have made her take up tennis.
FRAN. Right.
BIRDIE. She didn't have to play.
FRAN. Right.
HANK. I don't think she ever wanted to play.
VICKY. You don't know that.
FRAN. Right.
BIRDIE. Sometimes I think you did this to hurt us.
FRAN. *(Beat.)* Wrong, Roberta.
VICKY. You are so unfair.
BIRDIE. It's not about being "fair," Vicky.
HANK. Feel free to jump in here at anytime, Fran.
FRAN. I guess you're each entitled to your own opinions on the subject.
HANK. We're hoping for you to shed a little light on the matter.
BIRDIE. What happened, Mother?
FRAN. I was careless, Birdie. I am so sorry. I didn't mean to hurt any of you.
HANK. But you did.
FRAN. Right. *(The psychiatrists enter as the television flies off.)*
PSYCHIATRIST #1. What's your attraction to the soap opera, Fran?

FRAN. I hate that I watch it. It's the lowest form of entertainment really. Dolly likes the stories; but they don't interest me much. There seems to be no logic to anything that happens.
PSYCHIATRIST #2. Then why do you watch?
FRAN. I like to study the actors.
PSYCHIATRIST #1. The actors?
FRAN. It's interesting how some don't know their lines and others have learned their lines too well.
PSYCHIATRIST #2. Which are you, Fran?
FRAN. What do you mean?
PSYCHIATRIST #2. Do you know your lines?
FRAN. Mmm. I think I used to know my lines exactly. I played my part to perfection — but right now, I feel as if I don't know whose story I'm in.
PSYCHIATRIST #1 and #2. Uh-huh. Hmm.
FRAN. *(Beat.)* Look, I feel like I'm under this pressure to fill the time with chatter when I'm here. To talk about myself.
PSYCHIATRIST #1. Do you have any dreams you'd like to discuss?
FRAN. I don't have any more dreams.
PSYCHIATRIST #2. You don't have to always talk.
PSYCHIATRIST #1. You can just sit.
PSYCHIATRIST #2. You can just sit.
FRAN. Yeah. And I can also do that at home for free. *(Nervous.)* To be perfectly honest, I think this is going to be our last visit.
PSYCHIATRIST #1. Last visit?
PSYCHIATRIST #2. Who are you going to talk to, Fran?
FRAN. I'm happy to talk to myself now.
PSYCHIATRIST #2. Really?
PSYCHIATRIST #1. Is that wise?
FRAN. I've come to like my own company. I'll be just fine.
PSYCHIATRIST #1. Fine?
PSYCHIATRIST #2. *(Somber.)* Fran, are you sure you want to say goodbye?
FRAN. Well, you'll come back if I change my mind, right?
PSYCHIATRIST #2. Hmm.
PSYCHIATRIST #1. Huh.
PSYCHIATRIST #2. Not necessarily … *(The sounds of a game show. The psychiatrists exit. Fran follows their exit, then turns upstage revealing:)*

Scene 5

The curtain being drawn. We see that we are at another care facility. This one has a large window that looks out on to the beautiful Arizona desert. Fran's replica lies in the bed with Dolly at her side watching television. Hank enters with briefcase in hand. Dolly immediately rises, startled. She turns off the television.

DOLLY. Mr. D. You never come at this time.
HANK. I was on my way to a client. They cancelled at the last minute so I thought I'd pop over early.
DOLLY. I see.
HANK. Sit down, Dolly. Watch your program. *(She does as he wanders over to Fran's bedside. Beat.)* Fran looks good. *(To Fran.)* Hey, Frannie. You're looking good today.
FRAN. Thank you.
DOLLY. Squeeze her hand.
HANK. What?
DOLLY. Squeeze her hand, Mr. D. When I squeezed her hand yesterday, she squeezed back.
HANK. Un huh. Really, Dolly. Go back to your program.
DOLLY. No, no. It was over anyway. Our story isn't on for awhile. Mrs. D. and I can't wait, right, Mrs. D.? There is going to be a wedding today. *(Hank notices some jars and cans of Ensure over on a table next to Fran.)*
HANK. Who's eating baby food in here? *(Dolly is slightly taken off-guard, then:)*
DOLLY. Oh, I give Mrs. D. a little food. She likes it.
HANK. Excuse me?
DOLLY. I was just about to give her some.
HANK. Fran can't eat, Dolly. *(Dolly moves to the table and opens a jar.)*
DOLLY. Oh yes, she can.
HANK. No, she can't.
DOLLY. You just watch. Beef stew, Mrs. D. *(Hank watches her skeptically as she raises a spoon of baby food to Fran's mouth.)* Here

you go, darling. *(She spoons the tiniest amount into Fran's mouth.)* Did you see her eat that? I think this one is her favorite. *(Hank is momentarily stunned.)*
HANK. How long have you been doing this?
DOLLY. For awhile.
HANK. *(Getting agitated.)* And you didn't bother discussing this with me first?
DOLLY. It takes a lot of patience. I didn't even know if she would respond.
HANK. You think prolonging this with a little baby food is what we want, Dolly? What Fran would want?
DOLLY. This isn't just baby food. I mix it with a special potion of herbs and other island remedies. I kept my own mother alive with this for months. And she was fighting cancer — much worse off than Mrs. D.
HANK. Do you hear what I'm saying? You have no right to be doing this!
DOLLY. *You* hired me to take care of Mrs. D. To see that she stayed well. And that's what I'm doing.
HANK. Get your things together, Dolly.
DOLLY. Think how badly I feel —
HANK. It's time for you to leave us.
DOLLY. I don't know how she was able to hide all those pills. Who would think to look under the kitchen sink?
HANK. I will pay you for the full week.
DOLLY. I thought I had all her medication in my control. I thought I was doing everything for her. I just can't turn my back on her now. You don't have to pay me. I just need to be here. *(She goes back to feeding Fran.)*
HANK. *(Exploding.)* Put the goddamn spoon down, Dolly! *(Startled, she steps away from the bed.)* This is not your decision. Do you *know* what a hell we have already been through?
DOLLY. *(Steely.)* You won't know hell until you don't have your wife around. *(Beat.)* You love her, anyone can see that, Mr. D. Hand me some of that liquid over there. *(He doesn't move.)* Come on.
HANK. Don't you understand anything I've been saying? Were you ever planning on telling me that you were doing this? Well? *(Dolly doesn't respond.)* What does your Bible say about the sins of omission, Dolly? *(Shakes his head and begins to walk across the room.)* You have so much fucking nerve, do you know that? Damn hypocrite is what you are.

DOLLY. Fine, you be angry at me all you want. You swear at me. You call me names. Mrs. D. needs to eat and I have to feed her. *(Hank, helpless, sits; Fran crosses and sits next to him; lights pull down to the two of them.)*
FRAN. I am hungry, Hank. I am. Oh, I know. I'm not exactly alive, but guess what, I'm not exactly dead, either. *(She laughs; beat, then serious.)* Look at me. Please look at me, Hank. *(Hank turns his head back to Fran in the bed.)* I'm not the same, of course. Not the old Fran. She's been gone for some time. But, I don't know. Maybe she should be gone. *(Beat.)* We used to dance so well together, Hank. Remember? We moved like one, didn't we? It was so beautiful being in your arms. I felt so safe. So taken care of. So important. *(Beat.)* Anyway, it's very simple now. I'm hungry and I'm thirsty. And I want to be cared for and loved. And sometimes I'm listening and sometimes I'm not, like always. But I'm here. We're here. *(Lights restore.)*
DOLLY. *(Dolly picks up some Ensure and moves toward Hank; beat.)* I understand how you feel, Mr. D. I do. And I'm sorry for all the pain you've been through. I truly am sorry. I ask for your forgiveness. *(Beat; he nods begrudgingly to her.)* Give me a hand, please. *(Hank shakes his head in disbelief.)* For Mrs. D.
FRAN. For me, Hank. *(Begrudgingly he rises and walks slowly over to the bed; she hands him the Ensure.)*
DOLLY. *(Continuing.)* Take that dropper. Just fill it a little and hold it to her mouth. She'll do the rest. *(He does as told.)* See, she likes it when you do it. You're a wonderful husband, Mr. D. *(He looks at her like she's crazy and hands back the dropper; he sits, exhausted.)* Good job, Mrs. D. It takes a lot of time, but we got nothing but time, right darling? *(She gives Fran a kiss on the forehead, checks her watch and then goes to the channel changer.)* It's almost three o'clock, Mrs. D. This is the day we've been waiting for. The big wedding day. *(As she presses the changer, we hear the sound of a phone ringing. On one side of the room, Birdie enters. On the other, Vicky, wearing an apron, enters. Fran sits and observes them both. The girls do not look directly at one another when they speak.)*
VICKY. Hello.
BIRDIE. Hi.
VICKY. Hi.
BIRDIE. Sorry, I just got your message.
VICKY. Did you talk with Daddy?
BIRDIE. No, why?
VICKY. He wants one of us to come down this weekend.

BIRDIE. *(Concerned.)* What's with Mom?
VICKY. He says she's doing okay in the new place. Something is going on but he wouldn't go into it. I think he wants one of us around.
BIRDIE. He has Edith.
VICKY. Don't be cynical, Birdie.
BIRDIE. Was that cynical?
VICKY. Yes. Anyway, could you please do it this weekend? I have a thing I promised I would do with Mazie. Brownie picnic. *(Beat; Birdie stands stunned.)* Birdie, are you there?
BIRDIE. Sorry.
VICKY. Can you go?
BIRDIE. Vic, I don't want to go back to Arizona.
VICKY. Birdie — *(They both sit, Birdie next to Fran who listens intently.)*
BIRDIE. I don't want to look at her like that anymore. I can't get that image of her in that bed out of my mind. That's not how I want to remember Mom. You know what I mean?
VICKY. *(Beat; maternal.)* I thought you wanted to be there when she died.
BIRDIE. I know. *(Beat.)* I guess I don't know. I suddenly feel that's not what Mommy would have wanted.
VICKY. Well, Birdie, I happen to think she would want us to see her now. Look, we each have to do what we want. I'm certainly not going to tell you that you have to go. I'll visit after the weekend if I can.
BIRDIE. I'm sorry.
VICKY. Daddy'll be fine.
BIRDIE. I'll call him.
VICKY. Yeah. Maybe you'll change your mind.
BIRDIE. *(Beat; turning directly to Vicky; lights change.)* Vic, if only we knew.
VICKY. *(Turning to Birdie.)* If only we knew what?
BIRDIE. What was really going on with Mom. Maybe we could have done something for *her* before it came to this.
VICKY. You know, we did our best. *(Beat.)* And so did Mom.
BIRDIE. *(Without any conviction.)* Yeah?
VICKY. Call me.
BIRDIE. Thank you, Vic.
VICKY. Goodbye.
BIRDIE. Bye. *(Vicky and Birdie turn back out.)*
FRAN. Goodbye. *("The Wedding March" plays on the television. Fran*

stands and marches slowly upstage and looks out to the desert landscape. Hank, Vicky, and Birdie sit sadly with their heads bowed in thought.)
DOLLY. *(Tearful.)* After all Cassandra's been through. The car accident; the kidnapping; the rape. There she is, in that gorgeous dress, marrying handsome Damian. *(Fran turns and sits next to her replica.)* Sometimes things work out real good for people. Isn't it nice to see her have this moment, Fran? *(An enigmatic smile crosses Fran's face as "The Wedding March" comes to a conclusion. She lays her head down next to her likeness and the lights fade to black.)*

End of Play

PROPERTY LIST

Knitting
Television, remote
Prada bag with Blackberry
Coffees
Sponge, water
Newspaper
Paperwork
Christmas ornament
Bible
Clipboard, pen, forms
Checkbook
Jars of baby food, Ensure
Eyedropper, spoon

SOUND EFFECTS

Soap opera theme and dialogue
Phone ring
Car crash
Ringing
Period music
Noise from life-support machines
Dinner bell
Door slam
Game show
"The Wedding March"

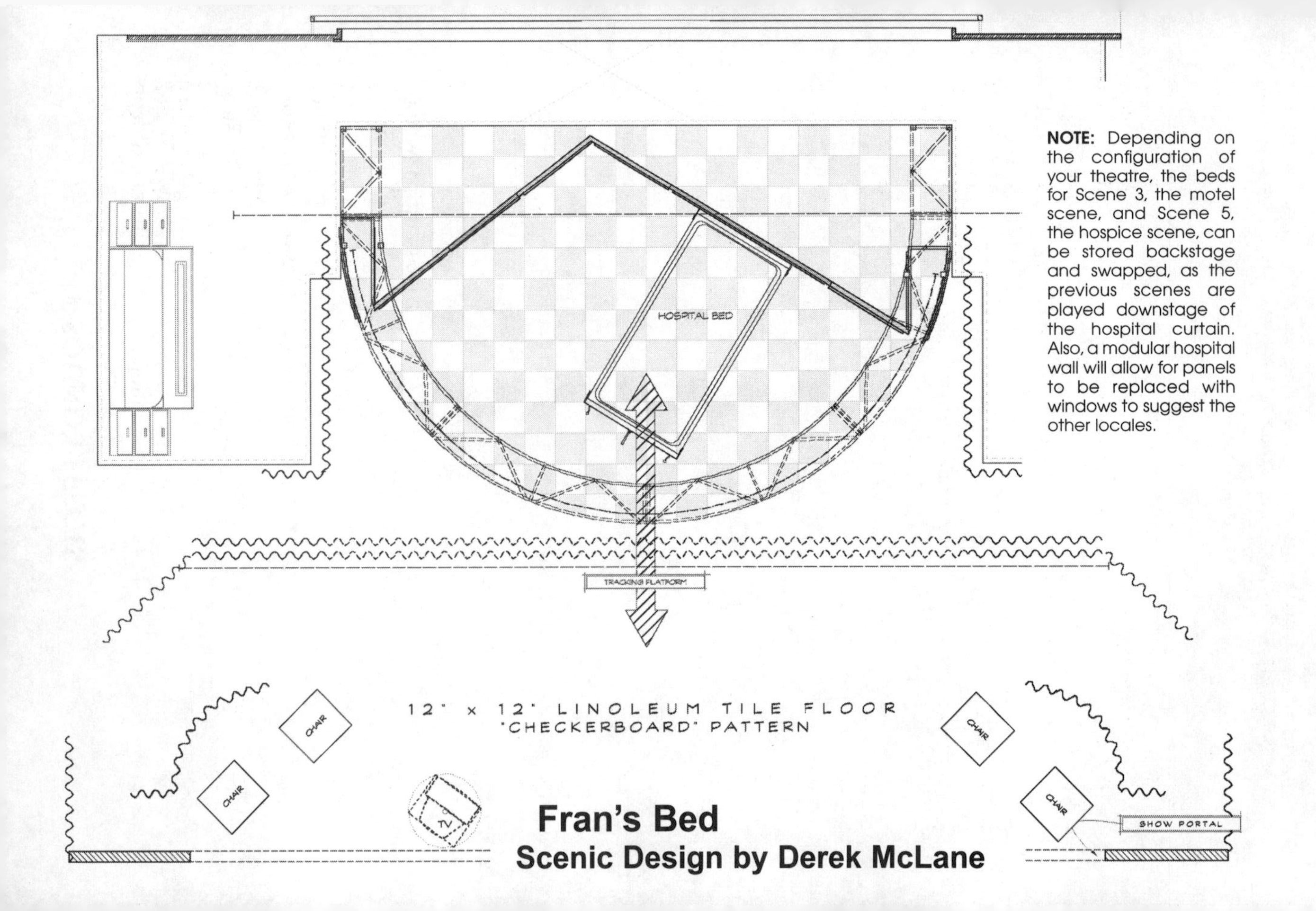

NOTE: Depending on the configuration of your theatre, the beds for Scene 3, the motel scene, and Scene 5, the hospice scene, can be stored backstage and swapped, as the previous scenes are played downstage of the hospital curtain. Also, a modular hospital wall will allow for panels to be replaced with windows to suggest the other locales.
HOSPITAL BED
TRACKING PLATFORM
12" x 12" LINOLEUM TILE FLOOR
"CHECKERBOARD" PATTERN
CHAIR
CHAIR
TV
CHAIR
CHAIR
SHOW PORTAL
Fran's Bed
Scenic Design by Derek McLane

NEW PLAYS

★ **GUARDIANS by Peter Morris.** In this unflinching look at war, a disgraced American soldier discloses the truth about Abu Ghraib prison, and a clever English journalist reveals how he faked a similar story for the London tabloids. "Compelling, sympathetic and powerful." *–NY Times.* "Sends you into a state of moral turbulence." *–Sunday Times (UK).* "Nothing short of remarkable." *–Village Voice.* [1M, 1W] ISBN: 978-0-8222-2177-7

★ **BLUE DOOR by Tanya Barfield.** Three generations of men (all played by one actor), from slavery through Black Power, challenge Lewis, a tenured professor of mathematics, to embark on a journey combining past and present. "A teasing flare for words." *–Village Voice.* "Unfailingly thought-provoking." *–LA Times.* "The play moves with the speed and logic of a dream." *–Seattle Weekly.* [2M] ISBN: 978-0-8222-2209-5

★ **THE INTELLIGENT DESIGN OF JENNY CHOW by Rolin Jones.** This irreverent "techno-comedy" chronicles one brilliant woman's quest to determine her heritage and face her fears with the help of her astounding creation called Jenny Chow. "Boldly imagined." *–NY Times.* "Fantastical and funny." *–Variety.* "Harvests many laughs and finally a few tears." *–LA Times.* [3M, 3W] ISBN: 978-0-8222-2071-8

★ **SOUVENIR by Stephen Temperley.** Florence Foster Jenkins, a wealthy society eccentric, suffers under the delusion that she is a great coloratura soprano—when in fact the opposite is true. "Hilarious and deeply touching. Incredibly moving and breathtaking." *–NY Daily News.* "A sweet love letter of a play." *–NY Times.* "Wildly funny. Completely charming." *–Star-Ledger.* [1M, 1W] ISBN: 978-0-8222-2157-9

★ **ICE GLEN by Joan Ackermann.** In this touching period comedy, a beautiful poetess dwells in idyllic obscurity on a Berkshire estate with a band of unlikely cohorts. "A beautifully written story of nature and change." *–Talkin' Broadway.* "A lovely play which will leave you with a lot to think about." *–CurtainUp.* "Funny, moving and witty." *–Metroland (Boston).* [4M, 3W] ISBN: 978-0-8222-2175-3

★ **THE LAST DAYS OF JUDAS ISCARIOT by Stephen Adly Guirgis.** Set in a time-bending, darkly comic world between heaven and hell, this play reexamines the plight and fate of the New Testament's most infamous sinner. "An unforced eloquence that finds the poetry in lowdown street talk." *–NY Times.* "A real jaw-dropper." *–Variety.* "An extraordinary play." *–Guardian (UK).* [10M, 5W] ISBN: 978-0-8222-2082-4

DRAMATISTS PLAY SERVICE, INC.
440 Park Avenue South, New York, NY 10016 212-683-8960 Fax 212-213-1539
postmaster@dramatists.com www.dramatists.com

NEW PLAYS

★ **THE GREAT AMERICAN TRAILER PARK MUSICAL music and lyrics by David Nehls, book by Betsy Kelso.** Pippi, a stripper on the run, has just moved into Armadillo Acres, wreaking havoc among the tenants of Florida's most exclusive trailer park. "Adultery, strippers, murderous ex-boyfriends, Costco and the Ice Capades. Undeniable fun." *–NY Post.* "Joyful and unashamedly vulgar." *–The New Yorker.* "Sparkles with treasure." *–New York Sun.* [2M, 5W] ISBN: 978-0-8222-2137-1

★ **MATCH by Stephen Belber.** When a young Seattle couple meet a prominent New York choreographer, they are led on a fraught journey that will change their lives forever. "Uproariously funny, deeply moving, enthralling theatre." *–NY Daily News.* "Prolific laughs and ear-to-ear smiles." *–NY Magazine.* [2M, 1W] ISBN: 978-0-8222-2020-6

★ **MR. MARMALADE by Noah Haidle.** Four-year-old Lucy's imaginary friend, Mr. Marmalade, doesn't have much time for her—not to mention he has a cocaine addiction and a penchant for pornography. "Alternately hilarious and heartbreaking." *–The New Yorker.* "A mature and accomplished play." *–LA Times.* "Scathingly observant comedy." *–Miami Herald.* [4M, 2W] ISBN: 978-0-8222-2142-5

★ **MOONLIGHT AND MAGNOLIAS by Ron Hutchinson.** Three men cloister themselves as they work tirelessly to reshape a screenplay that's just not working—*Gone with the Wind.* "Consumers of vintage Hollywood insider stories will eat up Hutchinson's diverting conjecture." *–Variety.* "A lot of fun." *–NY Post.* "A Hollywood dream-factory farce." *–Chicago Sun-Times.* [3M, 1W] ISBN: 978-0-8222-2084-8

★ **THE LEARNED LADIES OF PARK AVENUE by David Grimm, translated and freely adapted from Molière's *Les Femmes Savantes.*** Dicky wants to marry Betty, but her mother's plan is for Betty to wed a most pompous man. "A brave, brainy and barmy revision." *–Hartford Courant.* "A rare but welcome bird in contemporary theatre." *–New Haven Register.* "Roll over Cole Porter." *–Boston Globe.* [5M, 5W] ISBN: 978-0-8222-2135-7

★ **REGRETS ONLY by Paul Rudnick.** A sparkling comedy of Manhattan manners that explores the latest topics in marriage, friendships and squandered riches. "One of the funniest quip-meisters on the planet." *–NY Times.* "Precious moments of hilarity. Devastatingly accurate political and social satire." *–BackStage.* "Great fun." *–CurtainUp.* [3M, 3W] ISBN: 978-0-8222-2223-1

NEW PLAYS

★ **AFTER ASHLEY by Gina Gionfriddo.** A teenager is unwillingly thrust into the national spotlight when a family tragedy becomes talk-show fodder. "A work that virtually any audience would find accessible." *–NY Times.* "Deft characterization and caustic humor." *–NY Sun.* "A smart satirical drama." *–Variety.* [4M, 2W] ISBN: 978-0-8222-2099-2

★ **THE RUBY SUNRISE by Rinne Groff.** Twenty-five years after Ruby struggles to realize her dream of inventing the first television, her daughter faces similar battles of faith as she works to get Ruby's story told on network TV. "Measured and intelligent, optimistic yet clear-eyed." *–NY Magazine.* "Maintains an exciting sense of ingenuity." *–Village Voice.* "Sinuous theatrical flair." *–Broadway.com.* [3M, 4W] ISBN: 978-0-8222-2140-1

★ **MY NAME IS RACHEL CORRIE taken from the writings of Rachel Corrie, edited by Alan Rickman and Katharine Viner.** This solo piece tells the story of Rachel Corrie who was killed in Gaza by an Israeli bulldozer set to demolish a Palestinian home. "Heartbreaking urgency. An invigoratingly detailed portrait of a passionate idealist." *–NY Times.* "Deeply authentically human." *–USA Today.* "A stunning dramatization." *–CurtainUp.* [1W] ISBN: 978-0-8222-2222-4

★ **ALMOST, MAINE by John Cariani.** A cast of Mainers (or "Mainiacs" if you prefer) fall in and out of love in ways that only people who live in close proximity to wild moose can do. "A whimsical approach to the joys and perils of romance." *–NY Times.* "Sweet, poignant and witty." *–NY Daily News.* "John Cariani aims for the heart by way of the funny bone." *–Star-Ledger.* [2M, 2W] ISBN: 978-0-8222-2156-2

★ **Mitch Albom's TUESDAYS WITH MORRIE by Jeffrey Hatcher and Mitch Albom, based on the book by Mitch Albom.** The true story of Brandeis University professor Morrie Schwartz and his relationship with his student Mitch Albom. "A touching, life-affirming, deeply emotional drama." *–NY Daily News.* "You'll laugh. You'll cry." *–Variety.* "Moving and powerful." *–NY Post.* [2M] ISBN: 978-0-8222-2188-3

★ **DOG SEES GOD: CONFESSIONS OF A TEENAGE BLOCKHEAD by Bert V. Royal.** An abused pianist and a pyromaniac ex-girlfriend contribute to the teen-angst of America's most hapless kid. "A welcome antidote to the notion that the *Peanuts* gang provides merely American cuteness." *–NY Times.* "Hysterically funny." *–NY Post.* "The *Peanuts* kids have finally come out of their shells." *–Time Out.* [4M, 4W] ISBN: 978-0-8222-2152-4

NEW PLAYS

★ **RABBIT HOLE by David Lindsay-Abaire.** Winner of the 2007 Pulitzer Prize. Becca and Howie Corbett have everything a couple could want until a life-shattering accident turns their world upside down. "An intensely emotional examination of grief, laced with wit." *–Variety.* "A transcendent and deeply affecting new play." *–Entertainment Weekly.* "Painstakingly beautiful." *–BackStage.* [2M, 3W] ISBN: 978-0-8222-2154-8

★ **DOUBT, A Parable by John Patrick Shanley.** Winner of the 2005 Pulitzer Prize and Tony Award. Sister Aloysius, a Bronx school principal, takes matters into her own hands when she suspects the young Father Flynn of improper relations with one of the male students. "All the elements come invigoratingly together like clockwork." *–Variety.* "Passionate, exquisite, important, engrossing." *–NY Newsday.* [1M, 3W] ISBN: 978-0-8222-2219-4

★ **THE PILLOWMAN by Martin McDonagh.** In an unnamed totalitarian state, an author of horrific children's stories discovers that someone has been making his stories come true. "A blindingly bright black comedy." *–NY Times.* "McDonagh's least forgiving, bravest play." *–Variety.* "Thoroughly startling and genuinely intimidating." *–Chicago Tribune.* [4M, 5 bit parts (2M, 1W, 1 boy, 1 girl)] ISBN: 978-0-8222-2100-5

★ **GREY GARDENS book by Doug Wright, music by Scott Frankel, lyrics by Michael Korie.** The hilarious and heartbreaking story of Big Edie and Little Edie Bouvier Beale, the eccentric aunt and cousin of Jacqueline Kennedy Onassis, once bright names on the social register who became East Hampton's most notorious recluses. "An experience no passionate theatergoer should miss." *–NY Times.* "A unique and unmissable musical." *–Rolling Stone.* [4M, 3W, 2 girls] ISBN: 978-0-8222-2181-4

★ **THE LITTLE DOG LAUGHED by Douglas Carter Beane.** Mitchell Green could make it big as the hot new leading man in Hollywood if Diane, his agent, could just keep him in the closet. "Devastatingly funny." *–NY Times.* "An out-and-out delight." *–NY Daily News.* "Full of wit and wisdom." *–NY Post.* [2M, 2W] ISBN: 978-0-8222-2226-2

★ **SHINING CITY by Conor McPherson.** A guilt-ridden man reaches out to a therapist after seeing the ghost of his recently deceased wife. "Haunting, inspired and glorious." *–NY Times.* "Simply breathtaking and astonishing." *–Time Out.* "A thoughtful, artful, absorbing new drama." *–Star-Ledger.* [3M, 1W] ISBN: 978-0-8222-2187-6

DRAMATISTS PLAY SERVICE, INC.
440 Park Avenue South, New York, NY 10016 212-683-8960 Fax 212-213-1539
postmaster@dramatists.com www.dramatists.com